THE PARTY PRINCESS HANDBOOK:

An industry guide for all party character performers, from princesses to pirates!

M. Alice LeGrow

Philadelphia: PoisonApple Productions

PoisonApple Productions, Philadelphia, PA.
© Copyright 2015 M. Alice LeGrow. All rights reserved
ISBN 978-1-329-27921-6

Dedication

To Becky, who got me started in this biz.

To Julie, a great inspiration, mentor and boss.

And for my mom and dad, who continue to let me live the life I want, no matter how perfectly ridiculous.

The Party Princess Handbook

.

Contents

Prologue v

Introduction: Is This the Right Job for You? 1

Section One: The Basics... 5

    Chapter 1: Self-Assessment 7

    Chapter 2: Applying and Auditioning 15

    Chapter 3: Types of Character Performers 35

    Chapter 4: Beginning Your Bookings 47

Section Two: On the Job 63

    Chapter 5: Different Routines 65

    Chapter 6: Mascots 85

    Chapter 7: Large Events.. 95

    Chapter 8: Problem Customers 101

    Chapter 9: Legal Issues.. 105

    Chapter 10: Promotion and Making the

        Most of Social Media 113

Section Three: Resources and Maintenance...................... 119

    Chapter 11: Buying Costumes 121

    Chapter 12: Maintenance and Storing 127

    Chapter 13: Skin and Hair Care.................................. 135

Section Four: Emergency Index 141

    Your Emergency Kit.. 143

    Emergency Index 147

        Section i: Before the Party 149

        Section ii: In the Car.. 152

        Section iii: At the Party 155

        Section iv: After the Party....................................... 161

Closing   163

Acknowledgments.. 165

The Party Princess Handbook

Prologue

Supermarket openings, retirement homes...what's our next gig, a child's birthday party?

Squidward, *Spongebob Squarepants*

When I was a kid in the 1980's, one of my favorite movies was *Ghostbusters II*. I had the VHS tape and my little brother and I would watch it a lot, in between rounds of playing Mega Man on the 8-bit NES and wishing the internet was invented.

About the only part of the movie I disliked was near the beginning, when Ray and Winston are shown to be working part-time as birthday party entertainers. From the sad portable boom box they carry, to the jeers and insults of the children, the main message of the scene is that they have fallen from grace since the first movie. *This is what they've been reduced to,* says the scene. *Pity these once-proud men, for there is no more shameful occupation for an adult than that of a birthday party performer.* Even Ray's eternal sunniness and optimism, as he dons a party hat and accepts a slice of birthday cake, is seen as embarrassingly oblivious. He's enjoying himself, but we're clearly meant to feel awkward and sorry for him. As a child, I was horrified that my heroes were subjected to this kind of life and always thought to myself, "I will *never* take a job that humiliating."

The party performer as the punchline is a cruel but much-used cliché in entertainment. Aging singers, sad and talentless magicians, unhappy clowns, stars who have fallen out of the limelight . . . if television is to be believed, it seems that every one of them takes an eventual stab at backyard parties for kids. When Hollywood wants to convey that a performer has hit rock-bottom, inevitably that person is shown reluctantly working a birthday party gig. Party performing is apparently a visual shorthand for failure.

I take great offense at my job being considered rock-bottom. Forced rehab is rock-bottom. Trying to cook macaroni and cheese in a hotel coffee maker is rock-bottom.❤ Birthday parties are *fun*. And being a children's entertainer is the bottom of Hollywood entertainment in the same way that being Neighborhood Chairman of your local Girl Scout organization is the bottom of state legislature. They're not even in the same category.

Party performers are a special breed. We're part artist, part kindergarten teacher, part actor, part imaginary celebrity and part DJ. We pump the party up, do some entertaining, guide the kids through activities, kick out the jams, keep the dancing going and wrap it all up with a fun finish. Just because our party crowd is under three feet tall and wearing Spongebob sneakers doesn't make them any less great to entertain. The misguided visual of hard-to-please, disgruntled kids at birthdays is very rare for us. Kids are there to *party!* They're ready for fun! They want to dance and sing and play games and eat pizza and go nuts. And we're there to make sure it all happens.

But we do so much more than just party. We're also there to bring some magic into the lives of families who can't afford several thousand dollars to fly to far-away theme parks, or take expensive vacations. We're there for the kids in hospitals who can't go home for their own birthdays. We're there for disabled children who can't leave their homes and go to a show or a carnival, or who have special needs and require a one-on-one performer who will take the time to get to know them. We're there at charity events to help raise money for schools, hospitals and community centers. We march in town parades, greet kids at the local ice rinks and wave to crowds at park tree-lighting ceremonies during the holidays.

Most importantly, we're not in it for the financial rewards. Ask any veteran party performer and they'll tell you that they

---

❤ Trust me, it doesn't work.

endure low pay, sweating in costumes and the ridicule of just about everyone with a day job, because they *love the kids.* They love making kids happy. The sight of a child having their whole year made because you showed up to their party is what keeps this industry going. Sure, there are a few bad apples out there . . . the princesses who don't realize that "princess" is just their job title, not their actual birthright; the lousy performers who think a terrible routine is "good enough for a bunch of kids"; the owner starting up a cheap character company just because they think it'll be easy money. Every industry has some less-than-stellar members. But for the vast majority of us, doing it for the kids is what it's all about. Being surrounded by happy little smiles and knowing that you helped make their day is the best payment you can get from this line of work. We're not in it to be rich or famous . . . we're in it for someone other than ourselves.

And if nine-year-old me could see what I do now, I think she'd understand it and not be so tough on those Ghostbusters. Ray had it right after all: life's too short to care what other people think. Just put your party hat on and have some cake.

M. Alice LeGrow

INTRODUCTION:

IS THIS THE RIGHT JOB FOR YOU?

Did you know that for a few fleeting years, the Teenage Mutant Ninja Turtles were mascot characters at Disney-MGM? Not many people remember that. But I remember it. My parents had taken us on our one and only family vacation to Disney World in 1992, and at the emotional apex of our trip, my little brother and I met the Turtles.

We were huge fans, growing up overseas on a military base in Europe and playing ninja turtles with the other kids on the base. The sight of those turtle mascots, live and in-person, sent me into shock, and my brother into what I can only imagine was a child-sized heart attack. We mobbed those foamy costumes, got our pictures taken, collected their autographs and generally were of the opinion that life was all downhill from that glorious moment. Deep down, we knew they weren't real turtles. But when you're a kid and you see a character you love, reality and fantasy blur together in a weird way. Your brain knows it's not real, but your heart says it's the most real thing in the world. I hugged the costumed suit of Leonardo like the last lifeboat on the *Titanic*.

Fast-forward to today, and I am inside a turtle mascot suit, painstakingly handmade by me to an exacting standard of "just generic enough," so as not to infringe too much on the copyrights of my beloved childhood heroes, while still satisfying the Awesomeness quotient. I can't believe I've finally made this costume and actually get to perform in it. Originally

I volunteered to make it from scratch for a charity event, out of my own pocket, *just* for the thrill of being my favorite character. It wasn't cheap and it wasn't easy. I'd never even made a mascot before. But with weeks of research, saving for supplies and a lot of hard work, it was finally complete.

When at last the day came to wear it for the first time, my handler ushered me into the roomful of kids. I'd hardly gotten in the door of the venue before I felt a tugging sensation around my middle. Looking down through the quarter-sized eyehole opening, I saw a little boy hugging me around the waist as hard as he could, like he never wanted to let go.

Twenty-three years earlier, I did the same thing to another actor . . . and now here I was, in the same suit, as the same character, with a kid hugging *me*. It struck me that when I was the kid, I thought meeting my hero was the best feeling in life. Now that I was in the suit, I knew that sharing that kind of moment with this little boy was *really* the best feeling. Making a child this happy was better than meeting my heroes, or even playing them, and the strangeness of it coming full-circle from my own childhood made it somehow even better. It was hard to put into words just what I was feeling. I wish I could go back in time and tell the actor in that original turtle suit. He would have understood.

So with that sappy, feel-good anecdote out of the way, what exactly *is* the party performer industry?

First, a few things about what it isn't. It's not an industry for those looking to make easy money with little work. It's not for people wanting to launch their acting careers. It's not a clock-in, clock-out job that you drop the minute your scheduled time is up. It's not for divas and people who demand the spotlight. And obviously, it's not for people who can't handle being around kids.

But if you're the kind of person who loves kids and can talk to them even when they're upset, crying or disgruntled; if you're the kind of person who is responsible, always on time and never makes excuses at work; if you have offbeat talents and a knack for making people laugh; if you are infinitely patient, know how to keep your temper and can smile even through the most difficult and stressful moments . . . then you're the kind of person the industry wants.

Notice that nowhere in the above paragraph does it say, "drop-dead gorgeous." A common misconception, especially for princess performers, is that you have to be terribly good-looking to get the job. Although looks matter for some characters, the industry is not set on a seesaw of "beautiful" versus "take a hike."

Attractiveness and youth are on a spectrum, and what kind of job you want in this line of work will slide the requirements up or down that spectrum. Princess? Well, you should definitely be at least average-looking and somewhat resemble the character for which they're auditioning you, even if that means using a lot of makeup to do it. Mascot performer? You could be missing every tooth in your head and have five noses. So long as you can act well inside the suit and keep up your energy, you're golden.

A host of other factors are far more important than your looks. Possibly the most important factor is *are you good with kids?* Tolerating children or "thinking babies are cute" is not the same thing as being able to break up a tantrum, circumvent a pre-nap meltdown or draw out an incredibly shy child's inner party animal. Most party companies will prefer an average-looking performer who is great with kids, over a stunningly beautiful performer who can't control children at all.

My rule of thumb is that if you can't imagine yourself as a teacher for a day, dealing with minor squabbles, spilled drinks, endless annoying interruptions and potty breaks, then you are not cut out for the job. Because although we are entertainers and technically not required to act like babysitters on top of that, we always have to deal with problems at parties, since the parents hardly ever step in to help once our performance has started. It's up to us to keep the peace as much as possible. I've worked with performers who have stood like statues in corners at events, or chatted with parents while doing nothing to control the group of kids or lead them in activities. I can live without those performers, no matter how pretty they are, and so can the children.

As of the moment I write this, I'm heading toward my 34th birthday. That's considered an advanced age for the work that I do, which is mostly princessing. The majority of other character performers I know fall between the ages of 16 and 25. But I have a young face and even though I'm literally twice the age of some of my co-workers, my boss knows that I'm great with kids and I never let an awkward pause or dull moment interrupt my work at parties. The ability to keep your audience engaged, entertained and happy is more important than being the perfect age, looking the part, or owning your own costume.

Because we play characters, many fans of licensed characters want to join the industry. Disney fans, Marvel and DC cosplayers and others who want to "be their favorite character for a living" mistakenly believe that they can act out their fantasy in this job. It's only when they join up and find out that they're expected to be more like a teacher than a character, that they either quit or wise up fast. Party performing is not make-believe for wannabe princesses and heroes who crave the spotlight, the audience and the shiny costume. If you're getting into this job only to please yourself, look elsewhere. Once you put that costume on, everything you do is for the kids . . . from helping with crafts, to singing over a dozen shouting children, to cleaning errant sticky hand-prints off your outfit with a smile.

But if you really have the dedication, the determination and the motivation to make children happy, then you can succeed in this industry. There's a place for absolutely everyone of all shapes and sizes and all the eclectic talents they bring with them. It's a lot of work, but it's worth it!

So take a moment to read through the different sections of this handbook and see where your particular strengths lie. You may even find you have a knack for some jobs you never imagined yourself in!

The Party Princess Handbook

SECTION ONE: THE BASICS

You can't start working as a character performer until you get the job! Applying for a position with a party character company requires taking stock of what your personal talents are and translating them into potential character work, then putting all that information together on a résumé and querying your local companies.

The Party Princess Handbook

Chapter 1: Self-Assessment

Everyone has talent. It's just a matter of moving around until you find out what it is.

George Lucas

Time to get down to business and do an honest review of yourself as a performer. In this section, we'll do a self-assessment to determine your level of skill, your aptitude for certain character work, your unique abilities and what kind of role in party performing is best for you.

To start with, we'll assume that you're good with children. If you aren't sure you have this most fundamental of qualities, cross off all of the following statements that apply to you:

- ✓ I have babysitting experience (neighbors, younger relatives besides siblings, etc.)
- ✓ I'm comfortable around lots of smaller children.
- ✓ I actively engage smaller children in conversation.
- ✓ I don't lose my temper with children, even when they're being difficult or annoying.
- ✓ I genuinely like children and find them funny.
- ✓ I can relate to children, listening to what they have to say, instead of dismissing them.
- ✓ I don't "talk down" to children.
- ✓ I don't think children's problems are less important than adult ones.
- ✓ I know how to ask a child to do something in a kind, but firm manner.

9

✓ If a child gets unruly or upset, I can calmly talk them down without shouting.

✓ I'm not upset by a child sneezing, drooling or spitting up on me.

✓ I understand that children are often happy, sad, angry and scared very quickly in turn. It's just part of being a kid and I know how to deal with it, without becoming frustrated.

✓ People tell me I'm good with children.

If you've crossed off most of these items, or are confident that you could do so after a little practice, then you should be fine. That last item on the list is important . . . some people may think they're great with kids, but really aren't, while others who don't think so may be surprisingly good with them.

As I like to tell people, I began this job by just needing extra money. I was recommended to try it by a friend who is also a party princess. Even though I insisted I was no good with children, everyone who knew me said I was great with them. "You had them eating out of your hand," my dad said in amazement once, at a comic book library event I hosted for some kids ten and under. "You're like a kid-magnet," more than one manager has declared at most retail jobs I've had. "They just *love* you!" It wasn't until I really listened to my friends and family that I embraced this ability to create a rapport with kids and made it the focal point of my character performing.

You don't need to be the ultimate kid-magnet to work this job. Plenty of people start off more than a bit nervous around kids, but learn to love it. The most important qualities to have are:

Patience to deal with talkative, squirmy, or grabby kids, as well as shy kids who watch you from the corner but refuse to play, or bossy kids who want to hog your attention while everyone else gets pushed to the side. You can never lose your temper on this job, not for a moment.

Confidence to take control of the group and gently, but firmly, lead them through activities and routines, without letting everything descend into chaos. You must be a leader and make sure that everything is done fairly and peacefully, without arguments or conflict. It's your job to set the tone and pace of the activities.

Compassion, because kids are kids, not adults. They don't understand the world as we do. They make mistakes and don't realize it. They bump their head on something and cry for twenty minutes like it's the end of the world, only to stop immediately and be distracted by a colorful balloon. Remember that being kids doesn't mean their pain is any less than yours, or their problems any less upsetting. Something a parent might find hilarious, like a kid's pants falling down in the middle of a dance, may be humiliating to the child in question. Compassion will help you see the world as they do and understand their fears, their insecurities and their needs. Once you know that you have the intellectual and emotional skills needed to work with children on a regular basis, we can look at some other requirements for the job.

Are you physically capable of doing the work?

Something that doesn't often get brought up is the issue of the physical demands of this kind of work. A character performer skipping around and waving to all the children may look happy and at ease, but they're likely battling a heavy or restrictive costume, profuse sweating, uncomfortable shoes or the back pain of being asked to lift and hold 30-lb. children over and over for tons of photo-ops. If you have back and/or neck problems, difficulty standing for long periods of time, are highly susceptible to heat stroke or exhaustion, or don't have a lot of physical stamina, then this job may not be right for you. I was in a car accident about a year after I started my work as a performer, and even after physical therapy, I couldn't work a party for months. I still have trouble to this day because of lingering back problems, so I have to decline to lift children and sometimes turn down longer or more difficult events. It's not an easy job to do, unless you stay in shape.

The requirements of some jobs within party performing can limit the types of roles suited to those with disabilities. However, there are still roles available to those who have trouble walking or who have other difficulties that may keep them from actually playing a character. Face-painters often work seated and stationary, as well as do some balloon artists. There are also always positions for hosts and hostesses, who are assistants that set up the party items beforehand, act as a liaison with the parents or venue owners, help the character performer or mascot between sets, set up and hand out crafting or activity items, collect pay from the clients and clean up any party items or props before departure. Hosts can also double as face-painters at parties, or do small activities like glitter tattoos and nail-painting. Hosting is a very important job and a vital role for larger parties or events. You may be required to carry large plastic tote bins or rolling luggage full of props and supplies, but for much of the party you will remain seated and out of the way of the performance, so it's not as physically demanding.

Can you deal with the emotions that inevitably come from inter-acting with sick children, disabled children, dying children?

One very important aspect about being a character performer is that we do a lot of charity work. Party performers are sometimes hired to work at hospitals or other locations where the children to be entertained are disabled or seriously ill. More often than not, though, we're asked to perform on a volunteer basis at these places. No one will tell a company that they must do it. It's not a legal requirement. It's just implicitly understood that every company gives back to the community as much as possible and this way of thinking is endemic to the industry. We do it because it's just what we do. Every year, hundreds of thousands of dollars in free appearances, parties and giveaways are donated to hospitals, charity foundations and individual families in need.

What this means to you is that as a performer, you may be expected to volunteer occasionally for one of these events.

Nearly every performer I know jumps at the chance, even though they don't get paid anything for it. Who wouldn't want the opportunity to make a sick child happy for a day?

But many first-time performers aren't emotionally prepared for their first encounter with sick or disabled children. Some people who are great with healthy kids are conversely *terrible* with seeing children in pain. It's not something with which they can comfortably deal. When you do a hospital visit, you will inevitably be confronted by very sick children, some of whom will undoubtedly not survive their illness. If you regularly visit the same hospitals, as I do, you will learn not to inquire after certain patients you met the last time, because they may be deceased or transferred to another hospital for more specialized treatment.

It's a hard lesson to learn and some people may just know instinctively that they're not cut out for it. This doesn't mean that you can't be a party performer, but you should make your eventual employer aware of this and offer to help out with charity efforts in some other way – by distributing fliers, helping assemble gift bags, acting as a driver for other performers and so on.

You may also be hired to work with special-needs children on a fairly regular basis. Lots of families with special-needs children bring entertainment to their home because their child can't physically go to a theme park, has trouble socializing outside of the home, or has emotional limitations that make it hard for them to enjoy public venues. I've done parties for kids with Down syndrome, children with hearing and sight problems and even a set of three autistic siblings. You need to have extra-special patience, understanding and focus when dealing with special-needs children, who may be startled or afraid of strangers, or may need limited-stimulation activities in order to feel comfortable and focused. These are things you'll discuss with your boss when training for the job. For now, just be aware that it's something you may eventually have to do as part of your work.

Can you control a large group of children and speak commandingly, but nicely?

Are you naturally shy and don't like telling people what to do? Unfortunately, about half of a party performer's job involves telling children what to do, or asking them nicely. We never say the word "no" or give direct orders, but we are still responsible for making sure the children follow our direction. "Can we all sit in a circle now?" "Can everyone have a seat at the cake table?" "Can everybody get their listening ears on for the story?" "Can we all stand up and get ready to dance?" "Can we be quieter so everyone can hear the song?" We always phrase it as a question aimed at the entire group, but there should never be any doubt that it's a very gentle order, not a request. Children need structure, even at a party, which is what we provide: structured and planned entertainment.

Even if you're just at a meet-and-greet, waving and taking photos, you need to know how to tell a child what to do, if only for their own safety. "Can we please be careful with that?" is something you need to learn how to say to a child who is playing with sound equipment, or pulling at your costume and threatening to tip you over onto themselves, or making towards the table with the cake-cutting knife lying on it. You're not bossing children when you tell them what to do at a party. You're making sure that the event goes as planned and that all the activities have a time and place to happen, so everyone has the maximum amount of fun with the least number of mishaps.

Identifying your strengths and hidden talents

Nothing says "hire me immediately" like having more than one talent. If you can add face painting, dancing, singing, balloon twisting, speaking a second language or doing magic tricks to your résumé, you'll instantly make yourself a more desirable candidate for any company. So what do you do well? A lot of people will shrug and say "nothing." They may suggest hobbies, like gardening or biking. Many people feel they don't have any natural abilities that can help at a party or event.

However, I've yet to meet someone who *didn't* have some hidden talent that helped immensely. One girl I knew claimed she had no special talents at all . . . not singing, not dancing, not face-painting, not even organizing . . . and she felt pretty bad about it. But when it came time to make out some "Official Princess Certificates" to give to children at an event, she had amazing handwriting and signed the "Fairy Godmother" signature on the printed certificates like she was the Queen of England. Her ability to label gift bags and letters with beautiful handwriting was a talent in itself, and one that is surprisingly useful, as well as highly appreciated by parents who love those kinds of extra-special details. Another girl I know is amazing at inflating and knotting balloons. While we're still slogging through a packet of balloons in order to fill up the whole dance floor, she has her whole pack done in three minutes. She is a balloon-making *machine*. As for me, my talent seems to be making people laugh. I've always been a hammy little comedian ever since I was a kid, and making both the kids and the parents laugh at parties goes over extremely well for me.

Can you juggle, even just three balls? Can you sing pretty well? Do you have a knack for coming up with new and fun crafts to introduce to parties? Are you a cartoonist or have a talent for drawing caricatures? I used to turn down caricature work at parties because I'd never done it on the job before and felt I wasn't "qualified" to charge for it, until a friend pointed out that I'm not only an illustrator with nine graphic novels under my belt, but I also have a college degree in cartooning. I may have only done caricatures at college for class, but no one could possibly be more qualified to start trying it out for work than me. A lot of times we consider our talents not good enough to be used on the job, but you really never know until you try it out!

The Party Princess Handbook

Chapter 2: Applying and Auditioning

I'm a skilled professional actor. Whether or not I've any talent is beside the point.

Michael Caine

Auditions are easily the single most intimidating part of becoming a party performer, especially for first-time applicants. Let's face it, no one likes being judged, even to get a job. But auditions really aren't as scary as you might imagine them to be. For one thing, they're much more informal than they sound. Many party company owners will do auditions at their homes or at the central hub location where costumes are stored and performers change. You won't be standing alone under a spotlight in the middle of a vast stage!

So what can you expect to face when applying to a party company? In this chapter, we'll go over the basics of the application and audition process, before moving on to breaking down specific entertainer roles and the unique criteria of each one.

Applying To a Local Company

Obviously, the best way to find out which party companies are local to you is to simply do an internet search. Google the phrase "party company" along with your city name. If nothing pops up, try the name of the closest major city to you. There are thousands of companies around the world and almost certainly one or two within driving distance of you.

Once you've determined which one is closest, visit their website. Familiarize yourself with the kinds of services and packages the company offers. Look around to see if they already have application information posted. Many companies will either ask you to call them, or fill out an online form, or email them with your résumé and a few head shots attached. Many more companies may not have any job inquiry information available, *but that doesn't mean they're not hiring.* One of the biggest mistakes you can make is to assume that if there's nothing specifically asking for applications, then they don't want any. When I was first looking for character work, I sent emails to three different party companies in my area, using the customer email address on their sites. Not one of them had any application or job info on their website, but all three got back to me immediately after I wrote, expressing interest in hiring me. You never know until you ask!

Try to find out the name of the owner of the company before applying. It can usually be found under an "About Us" section of the company's website. It's good to direct your email to the owner personally and avoid the "To Whom It May Concern" cliché. If you can't locate an owner, address your email to the name of the party company itself.

A simple email directed to the company with the subject line "Inquiry about performer applications" is sufficient, along with content more or less to this effect:

> *Hello (name of company owner or business name),*
>
> *My name is _____ and I was wondering if you are accepting applications for character performer positions. I'm located in (your home town) and would very much like the opportunity to audition for your company. I have attached my résumé and a few recent photos. If you have a moment to talk, my number is (your phone number), or I can be reached at this email. Thanks very much for your time!*
>
> *Sincerely,*
> *(your name)*

That's all there is to it!

The two things you will most likely need to secure an audition are a résumé and some full-length photos and head shots. Head shots can simply mean nice photos of your face, taken by a friend. What the company wants is to know what you look like, if you have a nice smile, what body type you have and if it will fit the costumes they currently own. Even those applying for mascot work will need to supply a picture of themselves. So if you don't have any good photos of yourself, ask a friend to head out to the backyard and take a few for you in some natural light (tip: wait for a cloudy day as opposed to a sunny one . . . sunny days cast sharper shadows on your face). If you're in school or recently graduated, use a school photo for your head shot.

I used some pictures of myself in cosplay outfits and sent a separate nice photo of my face, taken by my roommate. Don't stress too much about not having professional photos to send, so long as the ones you have are clear, well-lit and recent.

Your résumé, on the other hand, should be carefully crafted to let your future employer see that you either have job experience involving a great deal of interaction with people or children (think customer service or day care work), or, if you're a student, that you participate in extracurricular activities. Things like drama, glee club, choir, swing, or other singing and performing clubs are ideal to put on your résumé. If you have any performing experience at all outside of school, or have worked with children at summer camps, Scouts, or church groups, include that as well. If you have sewing or mending abilities, be sure to point that out under your Special Skills section. Party companies always need *something* fixed and you'd be surprised how many people on the staff don't actually know how to sew!

A basic template to follow for your résumé can be easily found anywhere online. Here is the exact résumé that I used to get my first character performing job:

MARY ALICE LEGROW

Address XXX
Phone XXX-XXX-XXXX
Email: XXX@XXX.com

PROFILE

High-energy, dedicated performer with experience in character portrayal for promotion and events. Party game and activity experience, including face-painting, interactive storytelling and caricature art. Good with children, including special needs. Additional experience in costume design and repair, wig design and maintenance.

- Event, carnival and character photo-op experience.
- Public speaking and children's workshop experience.
- Ten years' experience as independent costume designer and seamstress.
- Assistant Costume Director at *Terror Behind the Walls* in Eastern State Penitentiary, 2011.
- Received multiple awards from national conventions for costume craft and performance.

RELEVANT EXPERIENCE

**2011 XXXX Fabrics, Inc., XXXX, Pennsylvania
Sales Associate**

Answer phones, direct calls, assist customers in-store, greet customers, advise on apparel design projects, manage fashion fabrics department, manage special orders customer database, manage framing customer database.

Awarded "A Cut Above" commendation multiple times for dedication to customers, friendliness and assistance beyond the requirements of the company when working with associates and customers.

**2008-2009 Music Training Center, XXXXX, Pennsylvania
Front Receptionist**

Answered phones, directed calls, managed client database, distributed mail, acted as liaison between management and clients, ran errands, performed light office filing and cleaning.

**2005-2011 Tokyopop, Inc., Los Angeles, California
Writer and Model**

Performed as a promotional model at large trade shows. Designed and illustrated fashion-oriented art books.

- Featured on MTV.com's "Overdrive" series as an independent costumer and model
- Designed and produced costumes for two-page spread in *Gothic and Lolita Bible*, Spring 2008 issue
- Designed and illustrated fashion pieces for limited-edition paper doll and art book
- Designed and produced costumes for promotional model use at international trade shows

**1998-1999 XXX Council For the Arts, XXXX, Connecticut
Intern/Receptionist**

Answered phones, managed client database, arranged class schedules, redesigned company logo, ran errands, performed light filing and office cleaning.

EDUCATION

- B.F.A. Sequential Art, Savannah College of Art & Design
- Published graphic novel illustration and graphic design. Featured in *Teen People's* "What's Hot" list, July 2005, for illustration and fashion design
- Proficient in popular image-editing software and computer tablet use; Adobe Suite; Microsoft Suite; OpenOffice; Various web design programs

References Available Upon Request

I didn't list all the jobs I've ever had, just relevant ones that I thought might interest a party company. I also downplayed what I mostly did for TOKYOPOP (write and illustrate a graphic novel series) and focused on the aspects of the job that would be more interesting to a party company, like costume design and filling in as a booth model on occasion. Granted, I had no real job experience with children at that point, but I taught some art workshops to kids over the years, and I ran the Spring and Halloween carnivals at my college for two years, providing entertainment for local inner-city children (including running some carnival games and performing as the Easter Bunny). As for my hobby of being a cosplayer, those awards I've won at various convention masquerades over the years looked very nice in my first list of bullet points regarding my skills.

You can see from this that you don't have to have a mile-long list of performance credits to make a good impression. Just be honest about your work, but try to emphasize things that you've done which may be of use to a party company. If you're a student with no job experience, swap out any jobs under "Relevant Experience" for school clubs and activities, or even sports.

Showing that you can work as part of a team is a good skill to have as well. If you're musically inclined, put down what instrument you play and whether or not you've been professionally trained on it (music lessons count for that). If you're under 21, be sure to mention whether or not your school schedule is flexible, especially on weekends, and if you have your own reliable transportation, i.e. your own car. That's a big bonus, because even though a lot of princesses are still in school, it can be very difficult for employers to have to work around their schedules and transportation limits, and bus routes really don't work at all for this business.

Most importantly, two things that you can get which will impress your future boss are criminal check and child abuse check clearance certificates. You must have them in order to work a job around children, and they are extremely easy to obtain. Google either one, plus the name of your state, to find an online government form that will let you quickly apply and pay for both. Usually it's about twenty dollars each.

These certificates are provided by your state once a background check is run on you, to make sure you have no prior arrests and are not on any child abuse registries, nor convicted of child abuse. Once your background check is run and found to be in good order, the state will mail you your certificates within about 2-3 weeks.

Being able to include the phrase "Up to date on criminal and child abuse clearance certificates" on your résumé lets your future employer know that you've done your homework and understand the business. They'll also be glad that you've gotten this step out of the way ahead of time, in case they want to start training you on the job immediately.

What a Company Looks For

I'm going to get this out of the way right now: the party entertainment industry is not looking for smokers. I can't tell you how many girls have complained to me that they were *perfect* at their interview, have a great voice, love kids and look so much like the characters, but still didn't get the job. They tell me this while wafting out the unmistakable smell of cigarette smoke, which they're not even conscious of, because they're so used to it.

If you're a smoker, you can't hide it, even with breath mints and body spray. Parents won't tolerate a character who smells like cigarettes, alcohol or strong incense or patchouli, in that order. The children will loudly point out the smell when you hug them, every time. It's just the way it is. So if you smoke but really want this job, I can only suggest getting on the patch very quickly and doing your best to quit, because most companies just can't hire smokers.

Other than that, there are very few definite restrictions. As I mentioned before, it depends on what position you want: mascots can look like anything and be anyone, so long as they fit the costume and are great performers. Face characters, like princesses, fairies, superheroes and other human characters have more specific criteria that differ from company to company. What one boss considers too short for a princess will be ideal for another boss' fairy character. One company may desperately need more minority performers for certain characters, while another will already have enough. It all depends on what's needed at the time.

In general, face characters should be of average good looks, or easily made so by cosmetics. A face clear of acne and scarring, with a nice, engaging smile and more or less straight, white teeth; no braces, retainers or glasses (contacts may be acceptable); a clean-cut, presentable appearance, free of unusual features like large-gauge earrings, piercings, or tattoos; symmetrical features and a fairly good profile; average height and build, with an average shoe size.

Most of the costumes are made to adjust to various per-formers' sizes, so you don't have to be a specific size or set of measurements to get the job. However, you should be within the range of what they can accommodate with their costumes. If they have performers ranging from a dress size 4 to an 8, then you cannot be a 12, because they won't have anything to fit you and it will cost a lot to have another set of costumes custom-made just to fit your measurements.

The best way to know if you're what the company wants is simply to remember to include head shots and photos with your email inquiry. The company will know right away whether you're a match for what they're looking for at the moment. So if you hear back for an audition, you needn't stress being a good physical fit. So long as you haven't fibbed with old, inaccurate photos, you're good to go.

What to Wear

An audition is not quite the same as a regular job interview, although it will definitely have aspects of an interview process. Because you will likely be showing off your talents in movement, you will need to dress in something other than a suit or business skirt. Loose-fitting clothing will help you out if your future employer wants to see you go through a little dance, or do a few routines there on the spot.

The key is to dress for movement, but dress nicely. For women, something along the lines of a modest dress with a skirt that allows movement, or a collared work blouse over comfortable pants, is ideal. Flat shoes or a very low heel are best, so you can move in them and not give the employer a false impression of how tall you are (which is something they will likely consider). For men, a nice collared shirt and khakis is fine, as long as it grants you a lot of movement.

Even if you're going in for a face character role, resist the urge to doll yourself up and try to look the part of a character. False lashes, tons of eyeshadow, a face full of pirate stubble and other character makeup have no place in an audition. A good boss will be able to imagine you with all of that stuff on, without you actually having to wear it. Just do your hair and face the way you normally would for a job interview.

If you have tattoos, be sure to wear something that will allow you to show them to an employer. Remember that you MUST point out any tattoos you have that might possibly be visible in a costume, even ones that you might not think would be visible, like lower-back tattoos. Plenty of bosses complain that they will hire a young girl in a long-sleeved dress, only to find out on the first day of work that she has a shoulder tattoo that can't be covered up.

Unless you're a pirate, most characters *cannot* have visible tattoos, and bosses would rather not be bothered with using makeup like Dermablend to hide them. It rubs off on the costumes and gets them dirty and stained, and isn't always foolproof. If you have a tattoo, it's not a deal-breaker, but be upfront about it at your audition and let the boss decide if it's going to be a problem. The same goes for piercings and other visible body augmentations.

What to Prepare

Preparing for an audition is all about knowing what position you want and what the boss wants to see. Some employers, when requesting that you come in for an audition, will tell you exactly what they expect you to do. But for many others, it's a pretty open-ended process, so it's up to you to prepare something in advance.

For princesses and other female characters, singing is a large part of the job. You don't need to be a wonderful singer, but demonstrating the ability to carry a tune, as well as being comfortable singing in front of other people, will take you a long way. I'm not a good singer, but I make up for it by practicing the same routine songs *constantly*, so that even if I can't sing anything else, I can sing what I have to sing for work, backwards and forwards. Practice really does help, as I've even gotten compliments from clients at parties on my singing.

Choose a song that's appropriate to your work . . . say, a well-known Disney song for a princess application . . . and practice it. It's perfectly OK to do a copyrighted song at an audition, so pick something you really like and that you know you can handle. Sing along with the recorded version of it, and then Google a karaoke track of it, with the lyrics removed, so that you can try it on your own. Most importantly, practice to sing for an audience, loud and clear. At my first few parties, I had a terrible time singing loudly enough for my boss' liking, because I was so self-conscious about my singing. It didn't help that the other princesses I worked with were all trained singers and much more talented than I am. But what helped bolster my confidence was practice, practice, *practice*. Now I can sing as loudly as I want at parties, because I know I have a firm grasp on the songs in my routine. I also made a CD of them and practice in my car on the way to every gig.

If you're shaky on your singing, just keep practicing the same song and eventually it will become second nature! You can also rehearse a little dance to go with your singing at the audition . . . something very easy and swaying that nonetheless keeps you moving and looking like a performer, not just a singer. (Check out "Chapter Five: Routines" for more info on how to develop your physical routine as a character.)

For male performers, it helps to practice a little spiel as if you're talking to an imaginary birthday child. Show the boss what you would do when confronted by kids at parties. I always do my Batman impression when explaining my job to people: I put my fists on my hips in classic superhero pose, stand up really straight, look down to about where a five year old's face would be below me and say in a booming, cartoony-heroic voice, "Well hello there, Tyler! I heard it's your birthday, and I came all the way from my city to make you an official crime-fighting hero, in honor of your special day! Tell me, how old are you? Wow, five years old? That's impressive! You look like you're on your way to fighting crime already!"

It's silly, but fun to do. And it helps you develop that slightly-campy, cartoon voice that kids like. If you're going to be Batman, don't be Christian Bale Batman. Be Adam West Batman. Be all the funny, tongue-in-cheek imitations of a "superhero voice" that the media loves to do. Strident, clear, authoritative and just a little cheesy. Be the kind of hero who will unironically say, "Yet another day saved! Evil will never again plague this fair city so long as I patrol it!"

The same goes for pirates and other characters! Don't be a historically accurate pirate, be a classic Peter Pan pirate, with lots of "arrs" and "me mateys" thrown in. Don't be a Prince William prince, be a Prince Charming prince. Kids love the more exaggerated characters. So choose your target audition character and go to town on coming up with a little staple introduction to use for kids, then show the boss that you know what to say and how to say it . . . and that you're not afraid to look a little silly in public!

Mascots are a different story at auditions. A mascot needs to sell their performance entirely with their gestures and body language, so smiling and speaking have no impact on their routine, although they're excellent skills to have for the basic interview portion.

You can show off your mascot skills best to potential employers by renting a cheap mascot suit (or even buying a throwaway Halloween costume from online) and filming a short video of you doing your best routine, in your backyard or at a playground. Having a video or even a large mirror to help you practice emotions and movements while in your temporary suit is also vital to your preparation for the audition, so don't be afraid to put on that giant head and get weird in front of the camera! Watch the videos afterward to see what you can improve on.

There are plenty of resources online for watching professional mascots at work, and you can learn a lot from them. Any sporting event with a mascot, any mascot parade or theme park video is perfect to review and imitate for practice. Once you're confident enough in your skills, put a final short video together, no more than four minutes, for your audition.

You don't need to perform tricks and stunts. Just go through a quick two-minute cycle of gestures: waving, laughing, doing a little dance, and expressing a range of emotions like sadness, happiness, excitement, fear, and anger. Practice waving big with both arms and waving small, pulling your elbows in and just moving your hands. Hop and crouch. Spin in a circle. Do the twist or a wiggly swim. Show off a funny walk or jaunty skipping movement. These aren't things you'll necessarily do while on the job, but it's important to show that you *can* do them.

When it's all done, you can either email your video beforehand to the company or bring it with you on a portable device to the audition, along with a CD copy for them to keep. Don't assume that they will have a mascot suit ready for you to perform in on the spot. They may not even bother to put people in a mascot at auditions, but they will love that you are prepared with your own sample of work to show them. (To read more about mascot auditions, see the section "Mascots" in Chapter 3.)

Most of all, no matter what kind of position you're applying for, you must remember to smile, smile, *smile!* More than anything, the boss wants to see that you are comfortable with public speaking and singing, and that you can consistently look happy. It's easy to audition in front of one person, but some first-time performers crumble under the gaze of twenty kids and a dozen adults at their first party. Always speak clearly, look people in the eye as you talk to them and SMILE. Sometimes I feel like 90 percent of my job is just remembering to always smile. You don't have to grin like a maniac during your audition, but be aware of what your face is doing and make sure it's not slumping down into a blank look or a frown. So much of your job depends on your ability to make others happy and you can't do that if you're frowning. When in doubt, smile harder!

Attending a Callback

Most party companies I know will often hire right out of the auditions. But for bigger companies, a callback may be necessary.

A callback happens when many people audition the first time and the boss chooses a handful to come back in and audition again, so she can see her favorite potential choices all together and narrow it down to just the ones she wishes to hire. The same advice for auditioning applies for a callback, since it's mostly a repeat of the first audition. Remember to emphasize all your special skills and really rehearse a good routine for your character performance, to make yourself stand out from the rest of the applicants.

If you end up not being chosen, it's not the end of the world! Thank the boss for her time and ask her if she could keep your information on file and keep you in mind for any future work. Ask for and appreciate any critical feedback she may have to offer you on your performance. Quite often, a gracious applicant who shows a continued interest in the company will be called back at a later date for future auditions. And if the company loses a few employees, you'll be at the top of the call list to come in and apply again!

Negotiating a Contract

So the boss ended up liking you so much that she offered you a regular position! Congrats! Now what are you going to do about that contract she asks you to sign?

Luckily, a character performance contract really isn't a complicated affair that requires a lawyer to negotiate. Most contracts are put in place to ensure that you won't start up your own competing business on the side while working for the company, or offer discounted private parties to customers that would conflict with the regular company booking. Sometimes clients who want a cheaper deal will try to negotiate directly with the performer, offering to pay them directly and avoid booking fees with the company. But this really hurts both the company and you in the long run. It hurts the company because they're the ones who put the time into marketing and advertising to get those clients in the first place and they don't make any money if the client pays you directly. It also hurts you, because it gives you a bad rep that will get back to your employer and around to other companies. No one wants to hire a performer who will go behind their employer's back and undercut the business.

So a contract is put into place to protect both parties. It also locks in your starting wage and clearly defines what the company will pay for and what will be your responsibility. For example, a good company will offer to compensate you for any driving time to and from parties that exceeds a certain range from your house (say, ten or fifteen miles), plus tolls. The contract will also state whose cosmetics are to be used, if you're responsible for supplying your own shoes, and so on. There are many things to go over and you should read a contract thoroughly and make sure you understand every point before signing it. Don't be afraid to ask your boss for clarification on some issues, or ask that certain things be added in, like whether tips must be split with party hostesses, if you will earn extra pay for mascot work and how much, etc.

When negotiating starting wages, your results will depend greatly on your local market. A large, metropolitan business with tons of clients may start you off at $75 an hour. A small, rural community company may only offer $40. A good rule of thumb is to ask for $50 an hour to start. Generally, you may be asked to work one or two parties for free as initial training, but after that you should expect to start your regular wage immediately.

Exclusivity

One thing that party companies pride themselves on is having a following for individual performers. Many performers really own their role as certain characters and parents will often want to hire a performer they like and have had before. They also recommend the performer to friends who will ask specifically for that entertainer. After I first began blogging about my job as a party princess, my boss told me she had people who had read about me calling to specifically request me at their parties and who didn't want a substitute. Building up a following for a good performer ensures that clients will only want to book with you and not with another company.

Because of this, exclusivity is a matter you should definitely cover in your contract. Some character performers work for

31

different companies at the same time. Although I started out exclusive to one company, I was able to negotiate a non-exclusive amendment to my contract in order to pick up work with a second company that was just outside the territorial range of the first company, thus doubling my income without directly undercutting my first boss. But I only got this amended because I'd worked with my first boss for years and she knew that I would not prioritize my second company over her. Many companies will want you to work exclusively for them, which is pretty standard. If they spend a lot of time booking parties for you, advertising your work and trying to build up a following for you, the last thing they want is for you to then take that following to another company, leaving them high and dry. So be sure you have this part of your contract hammered out before you sign.

Finally, there is a non-compete clause in many party company contracts. If you quit this job, your contract may request you not to start up a competing company in the area for six months, or some other length of time. This doesn't prohibit you from going to work for a competitor company that already exists, but merely from starting your own company.

This is to dissuade people from pretending to join a company, taking in all the training and learning all their techniques and then using it to compete against them by opening a duplicate business in the area immediately afterward. There have been many documented accounts of performers applying for a job at a company, staying for about three weeks or until they examined how the whole business is run, where the supplies are purchased from, what sources are used for wholesale crafts, etc., then quitting and opening their own business right nearby. I've spoken with some company owners who have even told of competitors booking them for "fake" parties (parties for their own children, etc.) and videotaping the entire event, then duplicating that company's costumes, games and routines. It's a dishonest action and one that ends up costing companies a lot of business as well as peace of mind.

Non-compete clauses are tricky, because they are enforceable by law in some places, but not in others. Be sure you know exactly what your company is asking of you when they request that you sign a non-compete.

Starting Your Own Company

You may have noticed that this handbook focuses on applying to existing character companies, not on starting or running your own. The fact of the matter is that if you have no experience as a character performer, then you really shouldn't start your own business. Now that's not to say that some first-time performers aren't tremendously talented individuals, or not up to the task. But the plain fact is that 90% of all first-time small businesses *fail* within their first year, and that includes the party industry. There is so much that goes into a business that many first-timers don't realize, but could easily learn on the job by apprenticing themselves to another company first. Insurance requirements, registration, payroll, tax filing, marketing, advertising, managing overhead, supplies and transportation . . . the list just goes on. Spending a year or two in the employ of another company is a small price to pay for learning everything there is to know.

Every time a new Disney princess movie comes out, there is a small wave of "pop-up" companies that emerge along with it, looking to cash in on the popularity. These pop-ups, usually consist of one or two friends acting as face characters, who acquire some pre-made costumes from online and hang neighborhood fliers, advertising extremely low prices that undercut the existing character companies in the area. They fly under the tax radar, requiring cash only payments and never registering their business or reporting their income. Because they often lack long-term planning and investing resources, or because their proprietors are in this as an "easy summer job," they have to make do with poor-quality costumes and wigs, instead of being able to invest in custom-made stock. They lack the legally required performer's insurance, leaving them open to accidents and lawsuits. And because many are young people in high school or college, with little real-world business experience, their personal account-ability towards clients can be middling to poor.

Almost all of these pop-ups go out of business very quickly, due to the owners not understanding the magnitude of what they've undertaken. But the damage is already done by the time they fold: local character companies who have been in business for years are forced to drop their prices to compete with the unreasonably low ones set by the pop-ups, which parents will cite in order to try and get a better deal. Those parents who book the pop-up companies often experience lower standards of quality in costumes, performers, routines, add-ons and the overall entertainment value, which in turn reflects badly on all local character companies. A customer who has hired an incompetent princess is unlikely to hire another one next year, even one from a far more reputable company.

As for the pop-up owners, they experience extreme disappoint-ment because they don't know what they're doing wrong. They sometimes get hit with Cease and Desist orders for using copyrighted names and characters, they receive poor online reviews from parents, and their low prices come back to bite them when their income turns out not to be enough to even meet expenses. A hundred dollars for a two-hour party sounds amazing to a high school student, but only because they haven't factored in gas, tolls, vehicle mileage, craft supplies, favors, costume cleaning costs, makeup and accessories . . . plus a dozen other things, including all the time spent in getting ready, driving, doing the event, and unpacking and performing maintenance on costumes.

At the end of the day, undercharging everyone else in the area for six months not only forces every other company to lower prices just to compete, it also leaves the pop-up company broke or just barely breaking even. They also run the risk of getting in trouble at tax time, when their unreported income and unregistered small business earns them a painful audit.

Worst of all, unreported pop-ups can't easily be claimed on future résumés as work experience. Because the business doesn't exist on paper anywhere and the only business reference is the owner herself, a large gap in employment is unaccounted for to future employers.

This is an all-too-common situation for companies that don't report their employees as such or for those who pay them under the table instead: you come up against a lot of legal problems like this that can keep you from proving employment or getting important government benefits. It also puts your employees in a bad situation, where they have to claim you as an employer, but don't want to get you in trouble for employing them illegally.

I will always *strongly* recommend that anyone looking to start as a character performer begin by apprenticing themselves to a reputable company in their area for a few years. Even if your ultimate goal is to someday own a business, you can't go wrong with first learning the ropes. It's a risk-free way to get all your training from an established and reputable source.

You'll find out just what goes into running this kind of business, as well as how to organize, delegate, manage, hire and book events. Plus, you'll be getting paid the entire time that you're learning! And if you're like me, you might eventually realize that you *don't* really want to own the business, but are far more content to simply work for a boss.

The party company owner gets a cut of the profits for a reason: they have to keep track of every single supply item, every event, every potential booking, as well as chase down unresponsive parents, do payroll work, sort out all the legal stuff, deal with angry customers and do all the headache-inducing paperwork late at night, when all the performers have gone home.

In addition, the owner almost never gets to actually perform at parties herself, since running the business eats up all her time. It's the number-one complaint I hear from party company owners who turned their profession into their own small business: they never get to actually perform any more.

I'm glad to leave all of *that* to my boss, and just get on with doing what really makes me happy: entertaining!

CHAPTER 3: Types of Character Performers

I used to be a Geico caveman for live events. I was a corporate mascot. It was the silliest job.

Eric Andre

Up until now, I've been throwing terms like "mascot" and "face character" around in this book. Now we're going to see just what the types of character performers are and how they differ. In Chapter Five, we'll look more closely at each character and how to develop a routine, perform on the job and other specifics for each one.

Face Characters

A face character is called so because you see and recognize their face, unlike someone encased inside a mascot costume. The name originated with the Disney parks, but is now recognized as a term for most character performers of a similar vein. Face characters include princesses, princes, superheroes, villains, fairies, pop stars and other humanoid personalities. They can be completely original to the company, based on public domain fairy tales, or be generic imitations of popular characters in modern media.

A lot of people consider this to be the most enviable position as a character performer, though it's a job just like any other and has its ups and downs. Face characters have the most pressure on them to look the part, to take good care of their skin and their physique, to apply their makeup perfectly and know their character's personality inside and out. A lot of times they have to sing, or speak with a specific character voice. They also have to smile constantly and to not let unavoidable things like sweating ruin a client's photos. And even though party companies are far less stringent in capping the ages of their face characters than they are at theme parks, you still age out of a face character role much faster than a mascot, mermaid or other types of character roles.

But there are lots of benefits for face characters, too. You have more opportunities to talk directly to the children, as well as more ease of movement. Kids *love* face characters and idolize their favorites, so you're always a hit at parties. Kids are also far less intimidated by face characters that they recognize, making it easier to win them over quickly. In the end, it all balances out between the positives and negatives, and being a face character is lots of fun!

Unfortunately, plenty of teens and adults *also* idolize certain popular media characters and wish to play them for their own amusement. Practically every audition that companies hold for new actors will include at least one Disney fangirl, who may not understand that our princesses are meant to be generic lookalikes and that her memorized Disney trivia and exact mimicry of Disney park audition standards will not help her, especially if she's no good with children. During the talks I give at conventions on how to get into the party character industry, I almost always get questions along the lines of, "Is there a lot of demand for so-and-so copyrighted character? Can I do that for parties? I really like that character." One fellow was extremely disappointed to hear that we don't get much call for Star Wars characters, and especially not storm troopers. He already owned the costume and really wanted to be paid to wear it, and kept insisting that there must be *some* market for it at parties. But he was missing the point: our whole job is that we supply what the children want to see, not what we want to be.

We are an industry dedicated to entertaining our clients, not ourselves. Playing dress-up as your favorite character is all right, but wanting to be paid just for that alone is not going to work. In this job, you will be asked to play many characters, some of which you may find boring or tiresome. But it's necessary to ensure that we have coverage for every event and it will help you grow as a performer. So just roll with it!

Pirates

Pirates are a type of face character, but have a category to themselves because they are more heavily influenced by historical sources than princesses, fairies and other fantasy face characters. Pirates are very popular for parties and pair extremely well with almost any other character: pirates and princesses, pirates and fairies, pirates and mermaids, etc. This allows the option of having a "boy and girl" team of performers to do a large event. It's no secret that little boys aren't exactly as thrilled with princesses and fairies as little girls are, but they really love pirates! So having both a male and female-targeted character available for an event helps capture the interest of the whole crowd. You can even do a pirates-only event with a pair of male and female pirate performers.

Party pirates, although drawing from history for their characters and props, are still very different from pirate reenactors. Party pirates must be pretty over the top and fun for kids to enjoy them. A five year old doesn't want to meet a scruffy guy in grimy clothes who is half-drunk and cusses a lot, no matter how historically accurate that may be. Even while pretending to be a rascal, your party pirate must be squeaky-clean in manners and conduct. History might also have to bend a little, to include a lot more empowered female pirates and friends than just Anne Bonny and Mary Reade (we do not employ or use the term "wenches" anywhere at kids' parties).

A lot of people think that being a party pirate is as easy as throwing on a swashbuckling overcoat, some big boots and saying "arr" a lot. But pirate performers actually do much more than just entertain with silly character antics. A lot of pirate parties feature the pirate imparting stories about famous buccaneers (appropriate for little listeners, of course) and a smattering of historical facts and funny trivia. They teach kids all about the different parts of a pirate ship, how to tell time at sea, what a doubloon is, whether or not pirates really had parrots on board, etc. They may also bring pirate-themed kid's books and read them aloud. In this way, they fill a niche between fantasy character and historical actor. It's a great and educational addition to any party lineup and children find it fascinating.

Pirates are also the foundation of a wealth of themed games and decorations. Almost nothing is off-limits to pirates in terms of copyright. Everything you think of when you hear "pirate" is in the public domain: parrots, palm trees, treasure maps, ships, the sea, gold and so on. It's almost too easy to come up with party favors, crafts and themes for pirate events, from coloring your own pirate flag to playing treasure hunt games. A pirate is the one face character who never has to worry about stepping on someone else's trademark. By simply drawing from some historical sources to create props, games and projects, you can easily offer a vastly entertaining and thoroughly original character.

What's important is to integrate some of those historical ideas with a solidly cleaned-up version of the actual pirate image. Clothes can't be dirty, but can be smudged with paint a little here and there to appear slightly worn. Outfits should be brightly colored and fun, not dingy, brown and washed-out like real pirates most likely wore. Emphasis of the character should be on adventure and sailing, not on stealing and robbing. Slapstick is a great favorite for pirate performers, since the character naturally lends itself to that kind of cavorting. And since pirates are rascals, they can talk with bad grammar and get up to shenanigans at parties (sneaking snacks in an obvious way to make the kids laugh, trying to eat a wax fruit, etc.). But they should do so in a child-friendly manner that is entertaining and non-threatening.

After the *Pirates of the Caribbean* franchise debuted, the industry had an influx of Jack Sparrow impersonators who wanted to work the party circuit. Many of these actors were extremely problematic to work with, not just because of copyright and because most four year olds don't know or care who Jack Sparrow is. Johnny Depp's Jack Sparrow is a character with a surplus of weird inflections and mannerisms that may seem charming to adults, but come off as strange and intimidating to children. Added to which, quite a few of these performers were in it just because they wanted to be the character, not work with children, and they showed it by getting really into their performance . . . to the point of hitting on our younger female performers and pretending to drink on the job. Some of them actually *did* drink on the job, if you can believe it. This just shows that we must be vigilant in weeding out the performers who are only in it to act out their fantasy.

Do not be a Jack Sparrow pirate. They may be great for adult parties, but not so much for small children. Think more "Jake and the Neverland Pirates", or "Muppet Treasure Island," both of which are fun, adventurous sources and most of all, child-appropriate.

Clowns and Magicians

Why would I put clowns and magicians together? Because they are two disciplines which cannot be lightly entered into just by reading this book. They're not only people in costume, playing a part like regular characters do, but they also have a highly developed set of skills specific to their own professions, which can take years to master. It would be foolish of me to try and cover in this book all that clowns and magicians do, when there are far better resources available to those who want to learn.

Stage magic has a million and one sources, both in print and online, for teaching you everything you need to know in order to start your career. The *Tarbell Course in Magic* by Harland Tarbell, first developed in 1928, has stood the test of time as one of the most comprehensive and influential teaching sources for magicians. At a staggering eight big volumes, you can collect them as you progress in skill and it's a resource no aspiring magician should overlook.

For those serious about getting into clowning, I would recommend the excellent book *The Art of Clowning* by Eli Simon, available at Amazon.com and other online sources. Simon is a professor of acting, a veteran clown and has garnered huge acclaim with his troupe, CLOWNZILLA. His book has in turn gathered a multitude of followers in the industry and is highly lauded by contemporaries of the craft. It's a welcome and valuable addition to any party entertainer's library!

There are also hundreds of online group resources and forums available to clowns and magicians that serious performers would do well to join. Take the time to Google around for some of the larger groups, as well as ones that are local to you. An active local community will support and encourage you as you learn.

Mascots

Who hasn't seen a mascot before? They're at the ball game, at county fairs, even at your town mall. Mascots are everywhere and are very popular with crowds and kids. Technically speaking, a mascot costume is any costume with a fake head, that covers your body almost completely. Mascots do not talk, relying on gestures and body language to communicate. Think Mickey Mouse, or the Philly Fanatic, or the Easter Bunny.

A lot of performers reading this book might erroneously skip over this section, assuming that mascots have nothing to do with the kind of work they really want, which is portraying princesses, pirates, superheroes, and so on. But whatever kind of character work you're auditioning for, it would serve you well to add on mascot work to the list of characters you're willing to portray. Even if the company you'd like to work for primarily focuses on non-mascot characters, they'll love to see a sample performance of you in a mascot suit, because it shows you have range and true dedication to your character work. I never knew how limited I was in my character work until I took on mascot gigs. Being forced to express myself only through my gestures and not with words really opened my eyes to just how much I depended on talking to sell my character. Now when I do character work, I'm more expressive with my gestures and have a much broader range.

Plenty of aspiring character performers don't know how to work in mascot suits. If you can do it, you're already a cut above the rest at auditions. And in this business, having as many varied talents as possible is how you get steady work.

A word of warning about mascots: when used by party companies, they can be great. But because Disney and other companies employ their own mascot characters, mascot costumes walk a much finer line between generic safety and copyright-infringement. They're also about ten times more likely to attract a Cease and Desist order than any face character. It's much harder to claim legal distinction from a cartoon or animal character, if your suit is pretty close to resembling the real thing in facial structure. Sometimes there's a little leeway for mascots employed only for charity and hospital visits, receiving no pay or compensation for their appearances, but for the most part, it's just not worth it to tempt the fates. Even buying a mascot costume overseas from China doesn't make it legal. International copyright laws may make it legal for them to create it over there and sell it, but it does *not* make it legal for you to use it here, whether or not it's for profit.

So if your company employs mascots, make certain that you understand what counts as legally distinct, and research which media companies are more lenient on letting people make generics of their characters, as opposed to which companies will come after you every time. A "wink wink, we all know who it's supposed to be" costume may seem generic enough to you, but pretty dead-on to an unamused legal counsel, and you might end up with a seven hundred-dollar giant paperweight that you've been legally forbidden to use. Play it safe!

(For more information on legal distinctions with characters, see Chapter 8: Legal issues.)

When considering mascot work, do an honest assessment of your fitness level. Are you healthy and free of anything that might prevent you from this kind of work (asthma, poor circulation, high blood pressure)? Are you active? Do you exercise at least twice a week? Can you walk briskly up three flights of stairs without feeling tired or winded? These are the minimum requirements just for party mascot work, which can be extremely grueling and involve dehydration, constant sweating and a minimal field of vision.

If your job is going to require you to be in a mascot suit every weekend for more than two hours a day, you need to be physically fit and should get into good shape before you consider auditioning. It can't be stressed enough that mascot work seems easy and is often taken for granted. But after you sweat a bucket of water out in half an hour and your body temperature is rising rapidly, you'll realize just how difficult mascot work really is. So be sure you're up for it!

Mermaids

Mermaids and other aquatic performers are a much rarer breed of character performer. You may not be as familiar with them as you are with mascots, but they've recently been on the rise in popularity for party and event booking. From the superstar performers like Hannah Mermaid, to the regular-joe party girls looking to book their fins at the local pool, mermaiding is an offshoot of character performance that is both very rewarding and incredibly challenging.

To start with, a performing mermaid must have extremely good insurance with her company. She must be an *excellent* swimmer, not a fair-to-middling swimmer, or a pretty good swimmer. Think lifeguard-certified swimmer, with the ability to hold one's breath for up to two minutes. Many performing mermaids are, in fact, certified as lifeguards and it's a standard in the industry to take courses and get diver certification. In fact, it's required by most aquariums and public tank venues that regularly book mermaids.

Do you *have* to have dive certification? Do you have to be a lifeguard? No. But it's strongly, strongly recommended. Mermaiding is not something you can just take up on a whim, or even after a few weeks of effort.

You need consistent training for many, many months and you will need to practice several times a week while on the job. You need regular access to a pool that will allow you to do laps in a costume tail or large monofin. You need to invest in a mermaid tail that could run you as much as $2,500, or have the technical skills to make your own. You need to be trained to swim on a monofin, and then in your tight, restrictive performance tail. If you're not an excellent swimmer and you're not trained properly, you could drown.

If you work as a party-performing mermaid, you'll be in people's pools at their homes, running even more risk. If a child is injured or drowns in the pool during your gig, you will be to blame. If you can't supply your own lifeguard for events, you are to blame. It doesn't matter who was really at fault once the lawsuits come flooding in. There are inherent dangers when you work around water and they are not to be taken lightly.

Added to that, a host of job hazards come with being a mermaid . . . constant skin, eye and ear infections, dry skin and brittle hair from pool chlorine, swimmer's ear, athlete's foot, yeast infections from being inside a hot, restrictive silicone tail for hours, muscle strain, back strain, ankle strain . . . the list goes on and on.

I have trained to be a mermaid performer and put a huge amount of time and effort into my training. I can honestly say that it's far, far more difficult than being a princess, or possibly even a mascot. Even though I'm a strong swimmer, I wasn't nearly up to the standards of a mermaid when I first started. And the initial equipment investment was staggering. So before your boss adds swimming mermaids to her lineup of characters, make sure both you and she have done the research, planned out the purchases and allowed for at least six months of solid daily training and rehearsals before even considering booking a gig.

There's so much to mermaiding that I simply don't have the space to cover it here, which is why I recommend that serious performers interested in this field purchase Halifax performer Raina Mermaid's book, *Fishy Business: How To Be a Mermaid*, available on Lulu.com. I own a copy of it and endorse it thoroughly as the best and most comprehensive resource available for aspiring merfolk to date. Raina's book is the gold standard for anyone wanting to get into mermaiding. Do yourself a favor and pick it up.

In addition, you can visit the fine merfolk at MerNetwork.com. The forums there are the best online for mermaid/merman professional work and you can find endless resources for tailmaking and purchasing, costuming, cosmetics, training, equipment, routines, certifications, or just moral support from the other performers and enthusiasts! I'm a senior member of the boards and have learned so much more from the Mernetwork than I could have ever found out on my own. So if you're serious about mermaid work, swim by and check us out!

Add-Ons

Many character performers work with talented individuals who provide add-on services, which are a source of entertainment for the event that is not the focal point of the main performance. These individuals are almost never exclusive to the party company that may employ them, but work as freelance artists for many different local companies.

Face Painters

Face painting is in high demand for almost every sizable event. Kids love it, parents get into it and it's an easy, portable attraction to set up in the corner without taking up too much room. Plus it's a great role for someone who may experience difficulty standing for long periods, as face painting is often done sitting down. Face painting is a skill that anyone can pick up quickly. Although there are lots of professional face-painters who can execute real masterpieces, there are just as many amateurs who can do a perfectly satisfactory job using quick techniques like stencils and gradient paints, letting them create impressive work very easily.

Because many character performers will pull double-duty as hosts or face painters for their companies, it's useful to have some face painting practice and skill when you apply for character work. The best way to learn is to buy a cheap set of face paints like Snazaroo (and *only* face paints, not acrylic or watercolor!) and practice on yourself or a friend. I actually recommend hitting up Youtube and simply searching for face painting tutorials there, as there are literally hundreds. It's the fastest way to pick up tricks, tips and skills that will make your paint jobs easier to execute. The fact that it's a video means you can watch along to see just how it's done. Best of all, it's free!

Balloon Artists

It ain't a party without balloons! Second only to face-painters, balloon artists are the most popular service add-on for

47

character parties. Balloon animals and balloon sculpture are skilled crafts that require a lot of patience, practice and a willingness not to jump every time a balloon pops. But the pay-off is worth it when you have an excellent balloon artist on your payroll. In addition to the usual dogs on leashes and butterflies, I've seen artists who can create Rock 'Em Sock 'Em Robot headpieces with moveable arms, for kids to wear as hats and duke it out with each other in balloon combat. Things like that can make parties especially memorable for kids. If you'd like to add balloon twisting to your skillset, take the face painting route and go on Youtube for free instructional videos that will get you started. You can also check out the following links:

http://www.tmyers.com – a balloon supply store web site that includes tons of free instructional videos.

http://www.balloonhq.com – for learning basic and advanced patterns.

Hosts

One of the most important roles in the party business is that of the host or hostess. Most parties just can't happen without a host to facilitate. Hosts are supplied by the party company and can be employees who only host, other character actors stepping in to fill the role, or they can even be the owner of the company. A lot of people who have started as character performers later transition out of the actor role and move into hosting for their company. It's also a great role for someone who doesn't necessarily want to be the performer, but still loves to work with kids and would like to work at parties and events. It has no age, appearance or height restrictions, so any able-bodied applicant is eligible for this position. Hosting does require some of the skills and characteristics of a party performer that we've already discussed.

The host is in charge of many things, including acting as liaison between the company and the client, gathering and bringing all the supplies to the event, blowing up balloons, setting out the games and crafts, often acting as face painter or supplying glitter tattoos, helping the performer, as well as a multitude of other functions.

Party companies can always use more hosts, so if you'd like to be involved in the party business without actually being a performer, applying for a job as a host definitely is worthwhile!

The Party Princess Handbook

Chapter 4: Beginning Your Bookings

Starting a new job is always scary, or at least for me it's always scary. It's like the first day of school.

Sean Maher

Congrats, you've got the job! Now it's time to buckle down and start learning the business quickly, so you can begin booking and making money. Since this job is quite different from clocking in at the office every morning, there are some things you should know first about what to expect.

At the Hub

To start, most party company activity revolves around the home base, or Hub. This location is where character performers come to meet and change, where hosts retrieve their daily supplies of games, crafts and paints, where all the costumes and props are stored and often where paychecks may be left for pick-up. The Hub is usually located at the owner's own house or in a rented business space. It may be as simple as a renovated basement, or as elaborate as a separate store-front, with a backstage area and a front shop space for hosting parties.

Wherever it's located, the Hub is where you will report on work days, to suit up in costume and apply any makeup or details. Your boss will give you start times for each gig (which is when you are expected to actually enter each party), but also may either build time into the schedule for your arrival and changing at the Hub, or require you to arrive at a certain specific time beforehand. You should know where the Hub is located, exactly how long it takes you to get there from your house (with and without traffic) and what the rules are for entry. Is it only unlocked at certain times or on certain days? If it's in a house, can you just walk in, or will that disturb family members? Is there a hidden key around outside? Find out exactly how you gain entry to the Hub and what that will mean for your routine. You may have to wait in the morning until the boss arrives to unlock the doors. Or she may leave the doors open and you can come and go as you please. Whatever the setup, be sure to give yourself plenty of time to arrive without being late, especially in light of traffic. "There was traffic on the way" is an excuse that doesn't hold water at most companies. Performers are expected to account for it and leave lots of extra time for travel, as well as check online sources for travel updates along their route.

Respecting the Communal Space

Inside the Hub, there will be a specific storage system for every item you use on the job. Costumes will be hung up, wigs will be stored and props will be sorted, all in their proper places. You will be expected to follow the rules of maintenance and not leave costumes on the floor, or accessories in pockets, or shoes strewn about. There may be days when you have to run back to the Hub and hurriedly change into a new costume for a second or third party, leaving no time to clean up. But always remember to tidy up your mess at the end of the day, when all the parties are finished. This is especially true of any cosmetics tables, which often become a wreck after half a dozen performers have messed about with them in the morning. Put things back just the way you found them, and it'll cut down on delays for everyone.

Be sure to always hang up your costume neatly and inform your boss if there are any tears, stains or damage she should know about.

Replace your wig on a wig stand or wherever you got it from. Collect up hair pins and safety pins, putting them all back where they belong. Put props and accessories away in their own bins. Remember, you're not just setting things right for your boss, but for all the performers who have to share the space with you.

It pays to get used to changing in front of others, since that's undoubtedly what you'll be doing. You'll often be expected to change in front of people of the opposite sex as well, so if you're shy, wear leggings and an undershirt beneath your costume.

A boss may require performers to wear tank tops or other underclothes, to protect the costumes from sweat and keep it from showing through while performing. You should also bring your own stick-on dress shields and adhere them inside the underarms of the costume to minimize any sweating damage. Just be sure to remove them before you leave for the day!

Costumes

Costumes are dispensed based foremost by character, then by size. Since most of the costumes will be one size fits most, a lot of lacing and adjusting may go into making the costume fit you. There will also be shoes that likely will be in a few standard sizes. They may not fit you perfectly, and if you can clear it with your boss to supply your own shoes, you'll avoid the pain of wearing too-tight shoes for the day.

Whatever you can do to prepare before you arrive will help get you out the door and to your gig faster, as well as take up less time at the changing station and the makeup mirror, so other performers can use them. Most people apply almost all of their makeup at home, and just do a few final touches with rouge and false lashes after getting into costume. It's also more sanitary to carry and use your own makeup, even if your boss provides some for you. It cuts down on swapping bacteria among performers.

You usually won't have more than twenty minutes to get into costume and you may not even get a chance to return to the Hub for a change later in the day, so second and third costumes may have to be brought with you in garment bags, so that you can change in the car or a bathroom. Be sure that you bring *all* the items for these later costumes, including matching shoes and props!

Makeup and Wigs

Applying character makeup is very necessary. I see a lot of posts online from younger party performers who say, "I don't need to wear makeup with my costumes, as I have a flawless complexion already!"

It's kind of a silly insult to insinuate that the reason all the rest of us are wearing makeup is to hide bad complexions. We're wearing it because it *goes with the costume*. If you have a large, colorful costume on, plus a wig, your plain and un-adorned face is going to look oddly washed-out in comparison, especially in photos. There will be a significant visual imbalance between your face the rest of you. When you see us troweling on rouge, it's not to look younger or prettier, but to help our faces keep pace with the costumes. It also helps us mold our faces to better resemble the character. I know when I take my wig off after a gig, I laugh at how overly made up and heavy-handed my face looks, with all that character makeup on it. But when I put on my wig without doing my makeup first, my face seems to shrink into the wig and my features look tired and less distinct.

For those reasons, makeup *is* essential and should never be skipped for a character. And since you're always being photographed by parents, you need makeup in order to make your features stand out and not get washed away by flash photography, bad lighting, or just a lousy camera. Even male characters can do with a few touch-ups of foundation to even out their skin and a darkening of the eyes and eyebrows with powder or liner, to make them stand out better.

If you're not confident in your makeup skills, ask another performer or your boss to help you. Just realize that you will be expected to learn quickly and do your own makeup, as others may not always have time to help you and do their own makeup as well. Character makeup tutorials online will help you greatly in learning how to nail down your look, as well as do tricky things like apply colored contacts and false lashes.

Be sure to use a lip liner pen and a brush for a nice, smooth lipstick application, and keep pieces of paper handy with you to blot your lipstick on in the car, just before entering parties. I always end up with lipstick on my teeth, so I make a habit of rubbing my tongue over the front of my teeth every few minutes during a party, while my back is turned to the children.

As for wigs, they're easily put in place and shouldn't move around on your head, so long as you remember to check the elastic straps in the back inside band of the wig. Little plastic hooks on the straps should connect to a row of tiny ribbon loops, allowing you to widen the wig, or cinch it smaller. Always use a wig cap to tuck your hair and keep it in place. I recommend open-top netting caps, as they're much better for your hair than the usual pantyhose-like caps. Avoid making your own hair into a ponytail or braid first, if you can possibly avoid it, as it creates lumps under the wig.

Put your wig on by holding it in the front center of the hairline with one hand and the very back center with the other. Apply the back of the wig to your head first, positioning it and then pulling down on the front to snug it into place. Once it's in place, check the back of the wig again and pull it down at the root, to make sure it covers all of your own hair. Little tabs on either side of the wig that correspond with where natural sideburns would be can be found underneath the hair. Pull on these and center the wig by adjusting them to right in front of your ears, so that the wig is centered. Always be sure to use matching-color hair pins to secure your wig. Even if you're sure it won't fall off by itself, put two or three pins in at the sides to prevent kids from grabbing and pulling your wig off mid-party. Make sure the wig hair doesn't hang in your face or get caught in your lip gloss. I recommend doing makeup first, then your wig. Otherwise you'll struggle to keep wig hair out of your face while trying to apply makeup.

An Average Day

During a day of parties (usually a Saturday or a Sunday), you can expect to do anywhere from one to five parties in a single day. I usually burn out after four, but I know some performers who regularly do up to six. However, the average is usually from one to three events per day. If you have multiple parties, remember to bring a bottle of water and some small snacks like granola bars and other portable sources of fast energy, because you'll get very hungry in between gigs! Many bosses discourage performers from eating while in costume, in order to protect the outfits from spills. So you will often eat in between changing for the next party, or throw a towel across the lap of your costume and eat only things that don't stain, like crackers or nuts. Meatball subs are not the best idea for a snack item.

You or the party host will have a list of all the clients for the day, their contact numbers and the name and age of the birthday child. This is essential, because greeting the child by name and showing that you know how old they're turning that day is standard for the business. Parents can also be antsy and will want to know when you're on the way, or just about to arrive, so it's important to give them a call.

A day of parties will include a few minutes of set-up at each event by the host, or simply a pre-announced entrance if you're by yourself. If it's just you, you'll have to call the parents a few minutes after you arrive and let them know you're outside, so they can get the children ready to greet you. After each party, a quick text to your boss will let her know that the party went well, that pay was collected or that you got good feedback. Then it's off to the next gig.

It's common for performers to either change in the car between gigs, or find a public restroom. Many's the time I've had to find a grocery store bathroom and hustle myself in with a second costume over my shoulder, emerging to the stares of shoppers. You need a very thick skin and a willingness to look odd in public, if you want to survive in this business. Luckily, as long as you give a big smile and a pleasant, in-character "Well *hello* there!" to people, they're almost always amused and happy to see you. It's rare for us to get spitefully heckled on the street. Adults like to see silly characters just as much as kids, and something unusual always brightens their day, especially if you give them a big wave and a smile!

More importantly, you must remain in character as much as humanly possible. Remember that as long as you have the costume on, you *are* that character to absolutely everyone, even with a second costume visibly in tow. If a child asks what you're doing in the local gas station, tell them you're visiting from your kingdom and wanted to see the town. If you have the time to stop and pose for pictures with kids who really want one, by all means do so. It may seem ridiculous to stay in character for a bunch of strangers who aren't even paying you, but you never know how many may be future customers. And every action reflects on your company, so avoid swearing, shouting or acting rude while in costume. Behave just as you would if you were at an event.

Keep cards for your company handy while in public and give them out to curious people, with your name and title written on the back of each card (for example, Princess Bethany or Pirate Josh). Referrals from employees can translate into bonus pay from your employer and lets your boss know that you're working hard to help with promotion.

On the Road

Using your own vehicle is a lot more convenient than being hauled around in the party wagon or the host's car, but you have to be prepared for lots of different situations which may arise. Always gas up your car the night *before* a day of parties. It's annoying to have to stop and get gas in costume and you'll tend to attract stares at the gas station while you're in costume. And if you're running late, even five minutes at the pump will seem like an agonizing cut into your travel time.

Every precaution must be taken to be sure that you arrive on time, or with time to spare. Lateness is not tolerated on the job and it is expected that if the boss said you will walk into the party at 3:00 PM, then you will arrive by 2:55 by the absolute latest.

Parents who have promised their child a visit at 3:00 don't want to hear you calling up to complain about traffic and giving a revised ETA of 3:30. It may seem trivial, but many parties include guests and family members who can't stay for the entire party, but definitely want to be present when you arrive. There's also a small window of time during which young children stay happy and cooperative at parties, before they get tired and cranky and need a nap. And it's a very poor reflection on the whole company if you constantly arrive a few minutes late to every event.

In order to get there on time, give yourself a very generous window for travel. My *minimum* for a route that expects no traffic jams is an extra twenty minutes on top of estimated travel time, and I check MapQuest (which always seems to give much shorter travel estimates against my GPS, which seems more accurate). I also print a paper copy of the directions to make sure I know where I'm going, even if I lose GPS or phone satellite. I also include the parent name and phone number, child's name and age on the paper for reference.

Twenty minutes seems like a lot of time to kill, especially if you don't think there will be traffic. But I've yet to arrive at more than five parties with lots of time to spare. I always seem to need the extra time to get around traffic, to deal with unexpected roadblocks or to cope with weather. If it's close to rush hour or I know there will be traffic on the route, I automatically bump the extra time to 30 minutes or more.

Even if you arrive ten minutes early, that's a good ten minutes you can spend in your car, fixing up your costume or makeup and rehearsing songs or standard greetings. So always err on the side of being early!

Reimbursement

You should always keep receipts from tolls and gas for your boss, and for your own records. Your boss will usually compensate you for unusual distances traveled, as well as any tolls. As for yourself, you'll have to account on your yearly taxes for all the income you earn through this job, but you can deduct expenses like supplies and vehicle wear and tear. The government will allow an automatic deduction of 15 cents per every mile you travel for work, to cover the cost of maintenance on your car. So keep a good record of every single party you do and what the total mileage was for each day. I have a very small notebook on my desk in which I record every party, including information like the date, location, what I was paid, if I received a tip and how many miles I drove. At the end of the year, I can consult this book for my taxes.

In the Ranks

Working as a character performer means being part of a team. Many performers will have to work together at events, playing off each other's characters and providing synchronized entertainment.

Even if your character is a robot and your partner is a fairy, you will have to work as if you have something in common.

Don't ignore your partnered performer just because your characters are from different genres. Work as a team and help each other out when kids ask tricky questions, or the group gets unruly. Team players are vital to a party company and those who can't get along will quickly find themselves without a job. So remember that if you're dressed as a glamorous princess, the other glamorous princess in the room is no less important than you, even if their character is less popular with kids. Never order a partner around, but always ask politely if they can help you with an activity and maintain the image that you are the best of friends.

This should also extend to behavior outside of the event. Cooperation at the Hub makes getting ready easier, keeps the common areas cleaner and eliminates hold-ups or problems. It's also helpful to have a good relationship with the other performers when you need someone to cover an event for you, due to illness or sudden change in plans. When you've got a fever of 102 degrees, but you just don't want to ruin little Miranda's fourth birthday, you'll be glad to have a fellow princess to call for backup.

Partnering with Other Companies

Occasionally, a well-meaning event planner will book performers from your company alongside performers from *another* company, sometimes your direct competition, often without telling you. Nothing's more infuriating than arriving at an event to see some strange characters already there. Clients never seem to get the idea that we don't like to work with our competition. Financial rivalry aside, character performers are very protective of the photos that are taken of them on the job, because our image and reputation online depends almost entirely on these pictures. If you book us next to a terrible company with awful costumes and photos of both of us together start to circulate online, parents always assume we're both from the same company, and that those awful costumes are *our* costumes. Different companies have different standards and they hate to be mixed and mistaken for each other.

Worst of all are the penny-pinching planners who decide to save money on a character or two by getting a relative or friend of the family to play them, in a bad Halloween costume. I know a lot of companies who, while not exactly storming out of the party, will do everything in their power to distance themselves from that person and not be captured in photos with them. This may seem petty and cruel, but our digital media is our livelihood. When a customer sees a badly-dressed girl in a second-rate costume with our company tagged on Facebook, our reputation takes a nosedive. Added to which, we can't control the actions of performers who don't work for us. If someone shows up drunk, makes inappropriate jokes, is a terrible singer, or behaves badly in a public space, we can't stop them. And it reflects right back on our own company.

There have even been cases of unscrupulous rival companies taking joint photos from events and posting them on their own social media, passing *our* actors and costumes off as their own. It's an underhanded, unprofessional thing to do, but it happens.

Believe me, we don't like to alienate the poor girl whose uncle talked her into dressing up as a bargain-bin Sleeping Beauty, or the brand-new party company that hasn't been able to save up for good costumes yet. They probably feel extremely self-conscious among veteran performers who have expensive costumes and a killer routine. We will do everything in our power to be nice and friendly to them before and after the event, but for the sake of our company, we cannot be photographed together.

Beside all that, it's just hard to establish a rapport with a performer you don't know, or to decide what activities to do if your respective companies have completely different routines. Different companies have different modes of acting that they instill in their characters and we can't account for that. At best, we end up looking awkward and forced with each other, which does not make for a perfect party for the children.

If you find that you unexpectedly have to work with a rival company, be polite and accommodating by working with them in any activity, but discreetly try to get your boss' or host's opinion on whether you should be in photos with them, or whether your characters should be unusually busy on the other side of the event at all times. Ultimately that's a call only your boss can make, much like the angry call she'll make later to the clueless event planner.

Reporting Illness and Emergencies

Getting sick happens to all humans, but most especially to party performers. Colds and fevers abound in this profession, because we're around children and invariably catch any little thing they may be carrying. Much like teachers, we have a reputation for getting sick from little kids frequently. But unlike teachers, we see a different group of fifteen or twenty kids up to four times on weekends, meaning we're exposed to as many as a eighty brand-new children *every single week,* or three hundred and twenty new children a month, or *three thousand, eight hundred and forty different children a year.* That's a *lot* of potential colds.

I always like playing Cinderella, because she has long gloves that cut down on how much skin contact I have with the kids. But the fact that is no matter how protective your costume, children will hug you, kiss you, sneeze and cough on you and even wipe their noses on you. Sometimes they lick you for absolutely no reason at all. There's just no way to avoid being constantly exposed to illness.

Because of this, and because it's unthinkable to do a party while sick and risk infecting a child or infant, we have to be very careful to have backups in place for emergencies. The moment you feel a bit under the weather or a cold coming on, you *must tell your boss.* Working sick as a party performer is not just unethical, it's actually much harder than just showing up sick to your office or retail job. Your face looks bad, your energy flags, your voice sounds awful and your entire performance will definitely suffer. Everyone will be able to tell that you're sick and the parents will not be pleased. I don't even want to know what would happen if you barfed on a child. A lawsuit, probably.

Even if you really need the money, or you think you might get better by the time of the party, tell your boss when you feel something coming on. A backup must be put in place, just to be sure. I once had a cold come up the morning of the party itself. I felt fine the day before, but just a short time before the gig (halfway through doing my makeup for it, in fact), I was struck with a terrible stomach pain that later turned into a fever in a matter of hours. Luckily, my boss happened to have someone who could cover for me. Don't take chances . . . always report in the minute you feel sick, even if it's days before the party. Better to cancel and let someone healthy do the party, than to sniffle your way through a gig and later get a furious call from a mom who insists you made her child sick.

Moving Up in the Ranks

There's always room for advancement at a party company. New performers who dedicate themselves to their work and are diligent in promoting the company will find that they are given more bookings as time goes on. A lot of companies often have more performers on call than they do available bookings, so priority for work is given to veterans and the most reliable of the group. By always being on time, getting good feedback from clients and doing your best to work well with your boss and your co-workers, you can eventually become one of the go-to performers for the company and will get a lot more work, raises and priority gigs for your trouble.

Working for a Booking Agent

Some experienced performers will eventually take work from booking agents, who only book independent character performers and provide no costumes or training, as they expect you to already be trained and in possession of your own equipment. I have worked with agents who own large regional party companies. It's different from working for a local company, because you must supply absolutely everything yourself, including costumes, props, crafts, paints, music and a routine. The booking agent receives a request from a client and searches his performer lists to find one that lives in the right area and owns the right character costume. Then he gives them a call and offers the gig. The performer accepts and is given the client's contact information, in order to negotiate what kind of activities will be presented at the party, when to arrive, and so on.

Booking agents pay more on average, because they have little overhead in their business. They don't buy or maintain costumes or props, they don't rent space to store things and they don't buy insurance for the performers. They just book the date and offer you the job. Because they have so little investment to pay off, they can afford to give you a bigger cut than a regular company would, because all of the investment is on *your* dime. You put in the time calling back and forth with the parent, you use your own equipment and spend your own money buying and replenishing craft items, face-paint and trinkets, plus performer's insurance and any travel costs, which both come out of your own pocket.

Booking agents can be a great source of extra income, but their reputations and reviews can be all over the place, due to their practice of contracting performers by word of mouth or recommendation, rarely meeting them in person and not giving them formal training. I prefer to work with an established local company that has a solid reputation, where I know the owner and don't have to shoulder the burden of negotiations with clients. If you have an interest in working with booking agents, be sure to clear it with your regular boss first and make sure it doesn't violate an exclusivity clause on your contract.

The Party Princess Handbook

SECTION TWO: ON THE JOB

Character performing isn't just a matter of showing up in costume and waving! You need to be skilled in improv, storytelling and acting for each particular character, as well as knowing the rules of the business and how to work with your specific company and its other employees. Your behavior and routine must be tailored for each event, from tiny household parties to large, community-sponsored appearances.

The Party Princess Handbook

Chapter Five: Different Routines

With improv, it's a combination of listening and not trying to be funny.

Kristen Wiig

Although the goal of every character performer is to entertain, different types of characters accomplish this in different ways. In this chapter, we'll talk about developing a specific routine for some of the most common characters and how each one will prepare for work, act on the job and improvise for different situations.

There are some behaviors that are universal to all characters. We do not say NO to children, or order them to do things, even in games. Instead we say, "Can you...", as in "Can you all line up for the next game?" or "Can you put your hands on your head for this part of the song?" or "Can you sit there while we get the pizza cut?"

We do not ask to use the bathroom at the client's house, or request food or drinks. Bottled water should be kept on hand in your vehicle and sipped from before entering the party. We do not comment on the state, design or cost of anyone's home, belongings or party supplies, except to declare them all perfectly delightful. We are polite to all people present and stay in character at all times, even when a parent tries to talk to us as a performer. If they ask us how long we've had this job, we tell them we've been a princess since we were born, or a pirate ever since we ran away to sea. If they persist, we politely excuse ourselves.

Most of all, we put our constant focus on the children, concentrating on making it the perfect party for them. We don't chitchat with the parents or wander off to sit down for a break in the corner, while the kids do crafts. We are always on the job, always making small talk to the children and always watching and encouraging what they do.

Aside from all that, there are some singular routines and mannerisms that each separate character utilizes. Let's look at a few.

Princes and Princesses

Royal face characters are fun to play and always a popular choice for party bookings. Due to the ubiquity of Disney's park characters, royal fairytale characters are the most widely recognized face of our business. They're what everyone thinks of when they first hear about our job.

Working as a party prince or princess may not be as difficult as working in a theme park, but it's still very challenging. For one thing, it involves very hot costumes, slow, deliberate movements and impeccable manners. For another, you must always, always, *always* be smiling. Parents snapping the odd photo while you work don't want to catch a shot of the princess not smiling. So you've really gotta work those facial muscles and constantly be mindful of how you look!

Princes, who are usually booked in the company of a princess and not solo, go a long way toward winning over the boys in the crowd, who may not be as delighted to meet a princess. Princes can help those solitary brothers, boy cousins and neighbors feel more at home at the party, giving them some high fives, asking what kind of sports they do, if they've ever done princely sports like horseback riding and so forth.

It's not necessary or expected for the prince to fawn over his princess and act in love with her. If anything, the chemistry between princes and princesses at parties is always treated as that of very good friends, not as an established couple. That can be a relief to some actors who don't wish to make imaginary goo-goo eyes with their co-workers for the whole party. It's especially a relief to me, as some of our company princes are literally half my age and we would both find that super weird and awkward. When arriving and exiting a party, however, the prince will always escort his princess out with an exaggerated gentlemanly air.

In general, a prince is dashing and a princess is graceful. Whether or not she's a fun, tomboyish character at heart, she's still usually mildly dainty and graceful during the party. This is done not to encourage old-fashioned gender stereotypes, but mostly *to keep the sweating down.* For a basic, unconscious bodily function that all humans have, sweating still somehow ranks high on the list of Things Parents Think You Should Be Able to Just Turn Off. I've seen parents complain that the princess' face was too sweaty for pictures, or her dress acquired mild leak-through spots of sweat by the end of the party.

People will complain about this even as they're reminded that they begged the princess to pick up all their heavy children in turn for pictures, or that they were required by their contract to turn the air conditioning on at the event and didn't.

"But it's a nice day!" they'll protest, while wearing shorts and a tank top. "It's not even hot!" And to them, it isn't. But put them in a heavy costume, makeup, a few under-layers and a dense, stifling wig and maybe they'd change their mind on that. I've had moms stand outside on a bright summer day in thin sundresses and talk about how it "really isn't that hot for this time of the year". . . while I'm standing two feet away as Snow White, wrapped head to toe in a thick velvet costume and pouring sweat.

The hotter your costume, the more you must try to avoid running, jumping or dancing too much. You can't stop and

71

blot your face or touch up your makeup in the middle of the party, so conserve motion. Instead of all-over body movements, we convey lots of movements in our arms, making sweeping gestures and lifted, open-palmed "royal hands." We don't dance wildly during music time, but sway back and forth and swish our skirts about with our hands, to give the impression of more movement than we're actually executing.

Princes and princesses never let their arms hang at their sides. Princes put their hands on both hips, fold their arms across their chests or lean nonchalantly against the wall, all while maintaining excellent posture and squared shoulders. Princesses keep their hands above their waistline as much as possible, clasped together at the chest, angled outwards in a dainty gesture at their sides or held together under their chin. They may also rest their hands neatly in their lap while sitting. During singing, they keep their hands moving to mark time, make gestures appropriate to the song, etc.

Doing laps around an event meet-and-greet is generally easier for a prince, harder for a princess. That's because the princess often has a large dress with a hoopskirt underneath, perfect for tripping on, knocking things over or bumping into people. A princess in a hoopskirt takes up the floor space of about two and a half people, so she must learn to compensate for that.

Hoops can be pressed at the sides to compress them so as to squeeze between people in crowds, or narrow doorways. When walking, your non-dominant hand should always be holding onto one of the hoops in the skirt at all times, to control which way the skirt swings and prevent tripping or bumping. Practice having a much bigger personal space and learn to allow extra room for it.

One main problem with hoopskirts is that they provide a tempting little "tent" for children to climb under. And yes, plenty of very small children will try to creep under your dress when you're not looking. You can't always catch and evict them, so be certain you have a good pair of white shorts or costume bloomers on underneath, worn over your stockings, at all times. I made the mistake of forgetting mine once at a party and during the dancing segment, a little girl suddenly emerged from my dress to announce that I was wearing Spongebob Squarepants underwear. Of all the times to wear my lucky underpants.

Royal face characters are a chore because of the hot costumes, singing demands and perfect manners, but their routine is very straightforward, with little to no improv required. Of all the party characters, I'd say they're the most scripted, so someone who is weak in improvisation, but easily picks up mannerisms and routines, would do well as this kind of character.

Pirates

Pirates, obviously, have a different set of mannerisms than other face characters. They can get away with being a bit louder and more boisterous, though not enough to startle or scare children. They can use the standard goofy pirate accent, as well as not-so-great grammar. And they can play little, harmless pranks on each other or other entertainers (tapping a person's shoulder from the other side to make them look, or picking up another person's hat and wearing it in a funny manner, etc.). And they can play up not knowing how modern technology works, or even what things like cars are. Those sorts of things make kids laugh a lot.

But pirates have to remember never to seem deliberately rude to anyone. They can pretend to argue over little things, like which is the best pizza topping, but in a lighthearted way, not a mean-spirited or aggressive way. Do the pirate swagger when entering a party, but tone it down when you get into the thick of a group of kids, or you might knock an unseen little friend over. Really get up there with your "arrrs" and "me maties," because kids love hammy pirates.

One inspiration that I actually recommend a lot is a couple of viewings of "Muppet Treasure Island." Not only is it a really funny movie, but Tim Curry and the other human pirates are the ultimate party pirates for me. I really love Curry in that role, because he's so close to what I think should be done for pirate captain performers. Give it a watch and see if you agree.

Fairies

Fairies are sort of halfway between princesses and pirates. They have the pretty outfits and wings to consider, but they possess a much more free-flowing, spontaneous personality and lend themselves well to improv at events. Fairies are often played with a much more childlike demeanor, showing great curiosity about "human things" and wanting to play more active games with the kids. Because their costumes are almost always much lighter and less restrictive, they can run, dance and jump without constant fear of perspiring. The only real danger is poking somebody's eye with your wings, which often have pointy ends, metal spokes or a thin, rigid framework. Practice wearing wings a lot and make sure the points of the wings are aimed upwards, not directed outwards from your back. You'll be less likely to cause injuries that way.

One problem that fairies frequently have at parties is being asked to fly. Although it actually comes up a lot less than you'd think, it's still something you have to talk your way around. Many fairies tell the children that they ran out of pixie dust that makes their wings work and most go home later to get more. You can also sell your character in "flight" by performing a lot of jumping and leaping that gets you some air time during your routine. If all else fails and kids keep asking this question, misdirect with a new game or activity.

Always remember that your wings will double your personal space and because they're behind you and out of your range of vision, they're even easier than hoopskirts to accidentally strike people with while walking. Practice well and make sure you have a handle on them before taking them out for a gig!

Superheroes and Heroines

Superheroes are fun to do, because you get to go *way* over the top with your character. I know that in this day and age of popular hero movies, you might want to base your performance on what you see on the screen. But believe me when I say that even if kids are fans of the media versions, they *want* you to be way more ham-handed with it. You have to get bigger than life and really have the hero swagger down.

Always aim for perfect posture, so you look tall and confident. Square your shoulders and hold your chin up, when not bending down to talk to kids. Fold your arms imposingly in front of you, or put your fists on your hips in Superman fashion. Stand with both feet evenly apart and focus your weight in the center, not leaning more on one leg or pushing one hip out to the side. Make your voice as full and rich-sounding as possible, so that it booms with authority (but make sure you're not shouting or speaking too loudly to shy children).

Superheroes and heroines often have more active games than most, which include a lot of physical activities. A few road cones and some blown-up balloons can help you do an indoor race, wherein the children hold the balloon between their knees and try to walk to the end of the race area without dropping it. Outdoor parties mean you can add hula hoops, ribbon dancers and other play items that tie into physically active games. Superhero Freeze is a freeze-dance variation where the children freeze into a superhero pose of their choice between the music. A small, foldable ball-toss carnival game can be put inside if there is enough room, with foam balls for tossing.

Get creative and active with your play during superhero parties. And always encourage kids to do super poses during their photos with you!

Hosts

Hosts obviously do not adhere to an entertainment routine like characters do. But they still have a great deal of work at parties and events, all of which must be done quickly and competently.

Here is a general example of how a host facilitates at a party:

At the start of every work day, the host will usually drive to the Hub and pick up all supplies for the day. This will often include separate tubs of materials for each party. The host may or may not also pick up the performers, and drive with them to the event. Some drive separately, but when a company has a lot of high-school or college-age performers without their own cars, it's easier for them to be dropped off at the Hub early in the day. They may also choose to drive themselves to the Hub and carpool to events, to save gas.

At the party or event, the host will go in beforehand to greet the client and review any last-minute instructions with them. The host will then bring in any supplies, crafts, games, face paint and other items needed for the event, setting them up for easy access. The host will often be in charge of determining in what order games and activities will occur for the party, and will have to decide what activities are most suited for each particular event. A parent may want to do singing at a certain time, or a special activity of their own, that has to be worked into the lineup. A child may have some disability that prevents certain activities, or might strongly prefer a specific game. It's up to the host to manage this information and then communicate it to the performer.

When everything is set up, the host will instruct the performer to make their entrance, re-entering shortly after them. The host will be in charge of encouraging children to listen to the performer, to sit in a circle, to line up for glitter tattoos, and to otherwise guide the children through all the activities. The host keeps the party on track and takes the burden off the performer, who must stay in character and keep the entertainment moving along.

Hosts often double as face painters, so they will sometimes set up a small table and chair with the paint supplies, off to one side of the party. They may also fill the role of photographer and use a staff camera to take pictures that are later emailed to clients.

At the end of the party, the host cleans up and packs all supplies, receives payment from the client and hands out any business cards, transports the supplies and performers back to the Hub, puts away supplies and/or repacks them for the next day and reports to the boss on how all the day's events went.

Hosts have to be very meticulous, organized and reliable in their work!

Activities

Activities are usually straightforward. Parents will expect singing, dancing, story time, games and maybe a craft or two. Themed crafts such as decorating a foam "magic mirror" with royal stickers, or coloring a castle drawing, are easy to do.

For the most part, I do some variation of the following activities:

The Wishing Game: I ask the children if they've ever wished on a star, or at a well, or thrown a coin into a fountain. Then I tell them we're going to make special birthday wishes today. I have a glass trinket box full of large diamond-shaped plastic gems (too big to pose a choking hazard) that I offer to all the children, allowing them to take one each. We do a little ritual of holding them in both hands and rubbing or shaking them, thinking about the things we want to wish for. Then every child makes their wish out loud (or a secret wish, if they're shy) and places their gem back in the box. I promise to take all the wishes back to my kingdom and throw them in our magic well, so they will come true. And my wish is always that the birthday girl or boy has the happiest of birthdays.

Coronations/Official Heroes: For princess or hero parties, you can do an official coronation with a small plastic crown to make the birthday child a prince or princess, or award a medal on a sash to the birthday child as a token from the Mayor of your Super metropolis making them an official crime fighter.

Add a lot of pizzazz to it, to really make it a spectacle. Present the crown on a velvet pillow and read a statement from a parchment, using a scepter to tap the child's shoulders. For heroes, let them take a Hero's Oath and swear to uphold justice and fight crime, then have them kneel as you place the medal around their neck and shake their hand. Always remember to encourage applause from the adults after the ceremony.

Musical Carpets: Much like musical chairs, but with dancing and six small foot rugs (shaped like crowns, or hearts, or stars). The rugs are about two feet wide and easily carried into the party by the hostess, and spread out around the floor. We dance and then jump on the rugs after the music stops. One rug is taken away every time the music starts up again. By the end of the song, we all try to fit on the one remaining rug.

Acting Story: Once at a party, I forgot my storybook to read, but the client was promised a story time. So I had the children stand up and spread out and I quickly improvised a story that I called "The Golden Bird," and had them act out all the parts with me. Acting along with the story has become so much more popular with my clients' kids that I now almost exclusively do acting stories, instead of reading from a book.

Singalongs: Self-explanatory. Nursery rhymes and other popular songs work well. Occasionally we would do an a cappella Disney song if it was absolutely demanded, but try to stay away from anything copyrighted.

Freeze dance: Easily done with a portable boom box and a remote, or a remote-control iPod dock-and-speaker combo.

Prince/Princess Says: Simon says, but with a name change.

Finish the Story: A round-robin version of a story that I begin and then pass along to the next child.

Pass the Toy: This one I did mostly with another company, never solo. The owner had the children sit in a circle and pass around a stuffed toy (usually matching the party's theme), while music played. When the music stopped, the child holding the toy had to stand up and either do a funny dance, or wish the birthday child a happy birthday. This was good for children who wanted to show off, or children who were shy and wanted to opt out.

Crafts: Something easily done with a host or by yourself. We would clear table space and provide pre-cut foam shapes of masks, mirrors, pirate ships, etc., and dump a huge amount of tiny stickers on the table and let the children decorate the items. One owner provided foam shapes of picture frames, with magnets already glued to the back. She would have the hosts bring a portable photo printer and take all the kids' pictures with the character, one at a time. Then, while the party continued, the host would insert the camera memory stick into the printer, print off a 4"x 6" photo of each child and spread them to dry on a side table. When the kids were done decorating their picture frames, they would claim their photos and take them home for their parents to tape to the back of the frame, making a nice little picture to hang on the fridge.

Adjust the themes of your games and crafts to fit each character. Pirates should have pirate-themed items and crafts like a tiny treasure chest full of wishing coins, instead of wishing gems, or pirate ships or maps to color or decorate.

Super heroes are very easy craft-wise, as blank masks for decorating are readily available at the craft store, and even more cheaply bought in bulk online. Wishing boxes can be tins with a superhero logo printed on them, filled with shiny "power stones" from the craft store that match the tin's color.

Fairy crafts are similar to princess crafts and duplicate games and activities can be used for both. You can also go with a nature theme and work crafts involving leaves, flowers and butterflies into the party. Party accoutrement should be more green and natural, less pink and girly. Fairies are good outdoor party entertainers, especially at camps and wooded areas where you might naturally expect to find a fairy.

Possibly the one thing kids want more than any game or craft is just to talk to you, face to face. You will often encounter stammering children who grasp at questions to ask you, coming up short. They don't really have a question, most of the time. They just want to get your attention and see you talk to them. Bend or kneel down to meet them at eye level and smile as you answer them. Don't rush them or cut them off if their chatter starts to wander. Be patient, be a good listener and repeat things back to them, so that they know you understand. For example:

> CHILD: Princess, princess! I have a dog named Jeff!
> YOU: Oh my, you have a dog named Jeff? That's so wonderful!
> CHILD: Yeah, he's . . . he's brown and has spots!
> YOU: He has spots? What a cute dog he must be!

They love to hear their statements repeated back, as it shows you're really listening and paying close attention to them.

If they're too young to speak properly or are too nervous to make themselves clear, don't endlessly ask them to repeat themselves, as it will make them feel insecure. Practically anything can be answered with, "Oh? How *wonderful!*" How

Wonderful is the name of my party performer blog for a reason. I say it more than anything else on the job. It's a one size, fits all answer to lots of incomprehensible statements. If you say it with eye contact and a big enough smile, the child will be more than satisfied. Remember, they don't so much want an answer to their queries, as much as they just want your attention.

Substitutions

Always have a backup plan for parties. You may arrive with a bunch of active-play games, only to find out that the parent neglected to mention her daughter is in a wheelchair. Your boom box may break before the freeze dance. The children may be fussy, or too excited to sit still for a story, or a lot older than you were promised, making the younger-kid games you brought seem very boring to them.

Improvisation will carry you through a lot of these problems, as long as you learn to think fast on your feet and get creative. *Never* have dead air, or moments when you just stand there doing nothing. If your boom box breaks, do freeze dance by clapping loudly in place of the music. If your games are too active or hard for the group, substitute a story-time instead. If the children are too old, ask them to do a round robin story, which older kids always find fun, then ask the parents to put on music for dancing. The goal is to never pause or hesitate, but quickly change up your routine in a manner that makes it look seamless. If you want to do a story and then a jumping game, but the kids are too hopped up on sugar to hold still for the story, nix it and add in a freeze dance. Be flexible in your lineup and don't feel that you have one routine to which you must adhere for every party. Think of your routine as a grab bag of many options, which you will select and assemble into a lineup after entering the party, meeting the children and assessing their current state. I always do this evaluation while playing the wishing game, which is my opener. Kids enjoy making the wishes and I get to sit and speak to them in a group, so I can pick out who is fussy, who is shy, who is eager to play and who needs a little hand-holding during activities.

Controlling a Crowd

A vital part of working parties is knowing how to control a crowd. This is the single biggest deal-breaker that bosses look at when deciding whether or not to keep a new performer on staff. A good performer will be able to keep children entertained, confined to the play area, listening to the performer and cooperative with their fellow children. A bad performer will let a small squabble turn into an argument, tears and parents having to step in and break up the situation, while the performer stands awkwardly by.

Even though we're not babysitters, there are times when we need to act like it. And a character performer who can only do their routine games and activities as planned and has no ability to control or guide the children is not going to do well in this business. There will be times when a sudden tantrum is out of your control and must be handled by a parent. But by constantly monitoring the children as they go through activities, you can defuse problems before they happen.

Always refer to the children as your friends. I refer to children as "little friends" so often that it slips into my everyday speech now, like when I'm at the supermarket and tell my pals, "Watch out with the cart, there's a little friend in the way!" It's also a handy code-word for speaking to clients at parties, or on the phone, while children are listening. "My special little friend" is usually the birthday child.

It's always good to speak firmly and clearly to children, and to lay ground rules for both them and the adults. Children should be encouraged to listen. Adults should be nicely asked to "make a big space for us to play," i.e. stop standing in the way, trying to take pictures. Never order, but always ask, "Can you...?" when instructing children to do things. Don't waffle or say "um, er, uh . . ." when speaking, but make it obvious that you are the one in control of the situation. When something comes up, don't look at the parents, but step in and take care of it yourself, so the children know you're in charge.

I'm lucky, in that I have a strong voice which carries and I never have a problem with controlling a group because of it. I just *sound* in charge. But for those with soft voices, you may have to try harder. Constantly ask chattering kids to get their listening ears on, so they know they must pay attention to you. Don't threaten to stop the games if they don't comply, but don't move on to a new activity until you know you have everyone's attention. If you're seated and can't get everyone looking your way, stand up to make yourself bigger. Make eye contact with all the children so you have their focus.

If a child is being so disruptive that you can't control him, give a meaningful look to the parents or adults in the room and then glance at him. They will get the message and remove the child. Very often, a fussy or crying child is just overwhelmed by the party and needs some alone time to calm down and focus, before rejoining the games. Don't feel bad that this kid is "missing out" on a game, because it's far worse to let them ruin it for everyone else.

Some children lash out or hit when excited. I've been punched by little girls while dancing, just because they get so worked up by the party, music and other sensory experiences that they don't know how to control themselves and will prod and hit you while laughing, trying to get your attention. Grab them carefully, but firmly, by the wrist to stop them. Look them in the eyes with a smile and say, "Now, now, let's not hit, OK? No one should get hurt at a party!" Same reaction applies for kids pulling at your clothes, trying to grab at your hair, etc. They're not trying to be malicious, they're just excited and overdosed on sugar and fun.

If the child is hitting or hurting other children and your warning doesn't stop them, excuse yourself for one moment and get the adult client. Tell them that little Erica is getting a bit too excited and may need a nice, quiet spot to calm down. Hopefully you can manage to do this in a matter of seconds, while the children are distracted with another activity. Never do it in front of them, or within earshot of another child or guest. The child may have special needs and this sort of reaction to over-stimulation could be normal for them.

Remember that when you walk into a party, *you* are now in charge of the group. Parents will look to you for guidance on how everything is going, and they will be very reluctant to step in to intervene or help. Do your best to manage the group on your own, but don't be afraid to ask a parent for assistance if a disruption threatens to ruin the party atmosphere.

Misdirection

One thing older siblings love to do is try to poke holes in your character's story and interrupt the party by declaring you a fake. To them it's just a fun game and a way to prove their cleverness, but it can grind the activities to an unpleasant halt, if you let it. Sometimes a parent will step in and do damage control by removing the older kid, but more than likely they won't be nearby when it happens.

The best way to get around argumentative children or avoid an awkward question is simple misdirection. It's basically the equivalent of pointing and yelling, "Look over there!" and taking off at a run when they turn to look.

If you get hit with the dreaded, "I don't think you're so-and-so" or "you're not real," immediately fire back with a pleasant-voiced, "Oh? I don't think you're the real (child's name)! How can I tell you're him? Do you have a license I can look at?"

The kid will usually smile and shake his head, allowing you to quickly follow up with a stream of patter that will make him forget his original statement. "You don't? But you look old enough to drive! Are you sure you're not a driver? If you could

84

be a driver today, right now, would you do it? Where would you drive if you could go anywhere?"

The key is to use their question to segue into a series of increasingly unrelated questions of your own. By the time they've already mentally sorted out their answers to everything, you've moved on and are addressing another child, or starting a new activity that requires quiet during instructions. Many times they only challenge your authority because they want to see how you'll react. If you demonstrate that they won't get the offended reaction they're looking for, they'll drop the inquiry. I can often turn these kids into my biggest fans at the party, if I get silly enough with them. Learning their names and then constantly calling them out during subsequent activities ("Who knows the answer to this trivia? I bet CHASE knows it! Chase is so smart!") will either embarrass them enough into leaving you alone (without you looking like you did it on purpose), or will bring them around to your side.

Some children who believe in you will nevertheless ask awkward questions or constantly interrupt your routine. They want to have your attention so much that they will stand up mid-game and approach you while talking about nothing, getting closer and louder until they're practically shouting in your face. It's hugely frustrating, especially if you get an Actually kid, as I call them now. I was the Snow Queen at a library event once and I could not get through reading one single storybook line without a little girl in the front row interrupting me a hundred times with, "Actually, actually, princess, actually, actually, um, um . . . I've been to this library before." She would yell "actually, actually" as her attention-getting phrase and then meander off into some unrelated point, all the while standing up to get right in my face. She interrupted so much that her father took her out of the room for a talking-to, immediately started again when she was brought back and continued to do it while a librarian sat next to her and tried to unobtrusively shush her and keep her seated. The last time I saw her, she was being carried bodily out the library door by her father, still desperately yelling, "Actually, actually!" at me.

These are the children that will test your patience and threaten to take that permanent smile off your face, as well as ruin the party for the other guests. You can't shush them or tell them to be quiet, because you're the nice character. But talkative or noisy children can often be politely shushed by saying, "Can we all get our best listening ears on now?" and cupping your hands around your own ears as if to amplify sound. I do this a lot, when the group is getting too loud or threatening to go off-topic and break up during a game.

If you get a child who simply asks an awkward question a lot ("Can you do magic right now? Can we see some magic right now?"), just keep misdirecting by saying, "Of course, but *first*, let's make sure we do . . ." and swiftly move to the next activity. You can keep doing this right up until it's time to leave, distract them momentarily during your goodbyes and make a run for it.

If you get an Actually kid, do your best to get the parent's attention and have them shushed or removed. It's the only way.

Arriving and Leaving

Characters should never be seen arriving by car, if it can be avoided. Parking down the street or around the corner is standard procedure. A lot of times, the parents will promise to keep the child in the house so that your arrival is a surprise, but then will get so excited the minute they see you on the street that they fling the front door open or tell the child to look out the window. I think birthday parties exhaust parents so much that they temporarily lose their common sense.

Whatever the case, try to arrive at the house as carefully as possible, as well as depart that way. You can have a big goodbye at the doorway if the parents insist, but let them know in a whisper beforehand to take the kids back inside after you leave, not let them run around in the yard. Kids will follow you up the street otherwise, if only to see the "carriage" that you said dropped you off.

Keeping track of the time while at the party is always challenging, especially if you're performing and can't check your phone or see a clock. Making sure you're sticking to a schedule is important, because having a day of back-to-back parties means you can't afford to overstay at the first party and wind up late for the second.

I have a cheap little silver bangle bracelet that I wear with all my female character costumes. I got it on eBay and it has a silver glitter "gem" that flips open to reveal a tiny watch face. I can surreptitiously check the time whenever I like. If you can't wear a bracelet like this, you can always get a small keychain watch, which are about an inch long. Or just remove the wrist bands on a normal watch and attach it to a tiny keychain. Clip it inside the waistband of your costume, inside a jacket, onto your story time basket prop or a hundred other places, so you always know what time it is without having to ask!

The Party Princess Handbook

CHAPTER 6: MASCOTS

*The right costume determines the character, helps the actor feel
who he is and serves the story.*

Colleen Atwood

Mascot performers have it tougher than anyone I know. The
inside of a suit is extremely hot, stuffy and restricted. If you're
lucky, there's a tiny built-in fan inside the foam head that will
vent a little stream of not-nearly-enough cool air onto you,
while the suit itself usually smells like other people's sweat. If
you're unlucky, your costume is an older model with a heavy
fiberglass head, no fan or vent and it smells like a LOT of
other people's sweat.

On top of that, the costume body is often padded and puffy,
holding in even more heat and soaking up perspiration. The
hands and feet are clumsy and make it easy to trip or drop
things. The whole costume itself can weigh between 10 and 30
pounds on average, which doesn't seem too heavy until you
suit up and start overheating.

Mascot work is not for the faint of heart, or the weak of back.
It's an intense job that requires you to be in good physical
condition, able to withstand thirst and mild dehydration, with
the strength to constantly be moving, gesturing and wiggling
around in a larger-than-life attitude, without flagging or tiring.
I've heard plenty of stories of performers experiencing heat
stroke and tunnel vision towards the end of what seems like
easy routines. I've even been through it myself more than
once.

Luckily for party performers, we rarely have to do the marathon hours of performances that sports stadium mascots, theme park characters and other performers need to endure. But that doesn't mean it's not still difficult or grueling.

Getting a mascot position is very different from regular character work. Since their face is never seen and their voice never heard, a mascot has to speak and emote with their whole body. Gestures have to be bigger than life, emotions have to be exaggerated, and your enthusiasm and energy has to be at a constant 10. I once did a party with a girl who was the daughter of the couple that owned the event facility. They had bought a mascot costume from overseas and instructed her to do a meet and greet, alongside me as a princess.

When she entered the venue in the mascot costume, she simply walked slowly into the room and stood motionless in one spot, arms at her side. As the kids lined up for pictures, she made no attempt to greet them or even acknowledge their presence . . . merely put her arms out to hug them for each photo. When the event was finished, she slowly walked back out the main doors to change. It was hands down the worst mascot performance I'd ever seen. The owners could have put the mascot costume on a mannequin and had the same effect! Most upsetting to me was that the children were confused and a little disappointed by this display.

Your performance inside a mascot suit has to be engaging, fun and full of energy. This doesn't mean you have to be bouncing off the walls, but you should always be doing *something*, so that at no time are you simply standing stock-still like a creepy giant statue. Children will find you more approachable if you are waving and dancing, and less approachable if you are standing still, emitting a dead-eyed mascot stare. Nothing scares little kids faster than a mascot that doesn't move. So remember to ABC: Always Be Cavorting!

Although many party companies often have some of their regular character performers pull double-duty as mascots, they know that not just any regular employee will do. Usually, the task is reserved for certain employees who have the stamina and patience to put on a hot suit, as well as the talent for pantomime and expressing themselves through gesture alone (and for anyone who wants to earn some extra money, party mascots often get paid more because of the hard work). This is where your value as a double-asset to your boss will come in: you'll get double the amount of work if you can take over their mascot duties, especially since your looks or gender don't even matter once you're inside the suit. I've played quite a few male mascot characters for little boys' parties and it's a nice change from worrying about my lipstick smudging or my wig being on straight. Best of all, I don't have to compete with every other princess at the company to get the mascot gigs because very few of them are willing or trained to do it.

Working as a Mascot

If the company decides to employ you as a mascot performer, great! So what next?

You may mistakenly want to load up on snacks right before your event, thinking that you won't get a chance to eat again until later in the day. But a full stomach and heat stroke make for very poor partners and more than one performer has learned that wanting to vomit while inside a mascot head is a terrible feeling. Instead, eat a high-carb meal the night before, like pasta. Have a small snack an hour or two before your gig and a good amount of water. You'll need the hydration much more than you'll need the food. Resist the temptation to down energy drinks before a gig. Extreme heat and a stomach full of Red Bull is also an unpleasant combination.

And if it wasn't already obvious, NO ALCOHOL. The worst thing you can do is be buzzed on the job around kids, when you might stumble into or step on a child because of your limited vision. The second-worst thing you can do is be buzzed

91

on the job, inside your own personal sauna, with little breathable air and alcohol dehydrating your body. You might throw up, pass out, or both. Just don't do it.

It's important to be on time for all of your gigs, and to pay attention to exactly how the costumes you use are put together and assembled on an actor. Know how to get into and out of your costume by yourself as much as possible. Don't rely on others to help you, because there will always be that one event when an assistant doesn't show up and you have no one to help you change. If you have to have help with one part, be sure you always know where your helper is at least fifteen minutes before you have to get in costume. Give yourself time to spare, in case there's a break in the outfit that requires quick mending.

Some things you must always bring with you to an event are:

- ✓A change of clothes for inside the suit (underclothes, t-shirt and leggings or sweatpants is fine, anything you don't mind getting soaked in sweat and can change out of later). Clients don't want to see you stroll out of the event soaked in your own sweat, so be sure to keep your street clothes dry for your exit.
- ✓Sweatband for your forehead (you WILL need one of these, to keep the sweat out of your eyes. You can't wipe away an eyeful of sweat if your hands are in the mascot's paws!)
- ✓Bottle of water or performance sports drink like Gatorade
- ✓Change of socks
- ✓Fitted sneakers (many suits require sneakers worn on the inside and don't have them built in)
- ✓A small towel
- ✓A duffel bag and a ball cap, to place your things in and to cover up a sweaty face and head when leaving, so as not to attract attention from kids
- ✓A spray bottle of cheap vodka (more on this later)
- ✓If you're a man, always wear an athletic cup. Trust me on

this. Nothing activates a ten-year-old's kicking glands like the sight of a mascot costume, and a five year old trying to get your attention is at exactly the right height to punch you in the groin.

While you're on the job, you may have what's known as a greeter with you, who is usually a host or other performer from your company. Since mascots do not talk (EVER . . . do not break this rule!), a human performer often acts as a greeter, leading children to the mascot, telling people what to do or where to stand for pictures, and generally greeting the guests before they interact with the mascot. It also helps when they can "translate" for you. Children often want to ask the mascot character questions, which you can't answer because you can't talk. I have played characters from shows who were accompanied by a human character friend from the same show, such as having a greeter as April for my generic ninja turtle mascot. The questions would be addressed to me in the suit, but the human "friend" would answer for me. For example:

CHILD: How come you came to my party, Mr. Turtle?
GREETER (as the human friend): Well he just loves parties so *much*! Especially the dancing! Don't you, Mr. Turtle?
ME: (nodding, giving a thumbs up and doing a little dance)

Children often don't mind the translation and feel that the mascot character is still answering them himself, even though he never says a word. It's important to have the greeter around to explain things to kids, let parents know what the mascot can or cannot do in terms of photo-ops, etc. They also manage the line for meet-and-greets. So if you can have a handler or greeter with you, so much the better.

While You're In the Suit

The ideal rule of thumb for a mascot performer is 30 minutes in the suit, 30 minutes out of the suit. So if you're at an event for two hours, you should only be in the suit for one full hour, with two breaks in between. You may go as little as 15 minutes a break, but you *must* take breaks. Remember that although you may want to impress your boss, skipping breaks to show off your stamina and dedication to the job is a bad idea, especially when the heat becomes too much and you ruin your company's reputation by passing out in front of a bunch of children. The breaks aren't just for your comfort alone, they're to ensure that your performance doesn't falter because of exhaustion. So if your boss sets a certain break time, take it and use that time to hydrate with lots of small sips of water.

Drink water on every break, even if you don't feel that thirsty. Avoid gulping it, but do drink it. If your boss provides a cold pack, put it on the sides of your neck, against the carotid arteries. This will cool your blood down much faster than placing it on your chest or head.

I hate to think that there are some bosses out there who may not offer you a break, but undoubtedly there must be. Some bosses may not think mascot work is grueling, or may have promised the venue owners a constant mascot presence for two hours. Don't get into a situation where no breaks are planned and don't go along with it because your boss said so. Your health is at risk here: it can't be overemphasized.

Establish before the gig starts exactly when and where you will take your breaks. It must be in a separate room or hall, out of eyesight of any children or guests. If the venue owners complain that they aren't paying for breaks, politely remind them that this is a health concern and that they don't want you passing out in front of their guests, then refer them to your boss.

The Golden rule of mascot work is NEVER REMOVE YOUR HEAD IN FRONT OF GUESTS. Even grown-ups. If they're not with your company, don't do it. Establish a safe resting room or area beforehand, away from the sight of the public and settle on a route to that area and a break schedule. Make sure your handler, greeter or boss will alert you to break times by finding you at the event and leading you to the rest area, deflecting any kids or guests who may try to follow.

Meet and Greets and Photo-Ops

When doing a line-up meet-and-greet (families form a line to "meet" the mascot character one at a time), a greeter is essential for holding the line, keeping people in check and admitting each visitor in turn. Without someone with the ability to talk, your line-up will instantly turn into a crowd of parents and kids, all pressing in on you and trying to get pictures with you at once, walking in front of each other's shots and creating pandemonium. Remember, parents get excited and lose their heads sometimes too, and they're always impatient to see that *their* kid gets the first picture. Nothing forms a mob of people faster than having no greeter to force them to line up and wait their turn. So make sure your greeter or handler is with you before doing official photo-ops and greetings.

Working a Room or Crowd

When you're out on the floor and mingling with the public, remember to be animated, but not terrifying. If there are lots of small children, keep your arms pulled in at the elbows. Walk very slowly and carefully, making sure you have a good enough field of vision to spot very small friends. Mascot heads are notoriously hard to see out of and you may be looking through a concealed eyehole as tiny as a quarter, so if you don't feel comfortable being able to see through the head, ask for a greeter or helper to guide you around the crowd and talk to children for you.

Do not sneak up on kids, even unintentionally. Children are startled easily and may become distraught at turning around to see an enormous creature looming over them. Slow, careful walking and small waving gestures to kids are best. If there's a group of children, circle around to a nearby open space and approach slowly from an obvious angle, waving, so that they can all see you coming.

When greeting a child, go for a high five, or pat them on the head or upper back. Hugging should be done with careful hands on their shoulders or upper back. Mascot hands are large and clumsy and in this day and age of lawsuits, it doesn't do to be accused of inappropriately touching a child, even when you're wearing the equivalent of two stuffed oven mitts on your hands. When I played the Easter Bunny for a charity event, a woman who was posing for the camera with me and her child suddenly turned around to me and asked in a sharp voice, "Hey, are you a *girl* bunny or a *boy* bunny?"

Apparently I had put my arm down to what I thought was the armrest of my chair, but was instead resting the gigantic furry paw on her backside. Since I couldn't feel anything through the paw and since my vision was limited to what was straight in front of me, I had no idea. But I couldn't very well take my head off and show her that I was a woman underneath and not trying to harass her. I had to make do with violently shaking my head and covering my face with my paws in a "woe is me" gesture to convey my apology. So be careful when approaching or posing with children.

Do not grab children or try to lift them. If a parent wants you to hold their very small child for a photo, try kneeling and putting out both hands to invite them to place the child standing on the ground in front of you. Or try walking to the side of the parent holding the child and putting an arm around the grown-up, and one hand on the child's shoulder. They'll get the message that you want to take the photo this way instead. If they insist you hold the child, crouch down to the ground as low as possible and try to let the child rest in your lap. Do not attempt to hold infants. Hold both paws up and do a little wave to the infant if it is offered, or get in close and pat the child's head gingerly and wave to the camera, but do not take the child in your own hands no matter what. Your costume hands are likely too clumsy to safely hold an infant and it's not worth the risk.

When facing children, do not tower over them. Bend or kneel down to get on their level so you won't appear so scary. Remember, you're in a big costume and you're twice their size. Imagine a 12-foot tall man in a lion costume is confronting you. It's intimidating! Try to get down low enough to look them in the eye, but keep at least three feet of distance if they seem wary or scared. Don't take it personally if a kid is afraid of you. Get down on your haunches and do a small, elbows-pulled-in shy wave. If this doesn't work, cover your face like a game of peek-a-boo and mimic shyness yourself. If this also fails, give them another wave goodbye and walk away. Don't try to force a child to be entertained, just to boost your own ego as a performer. Some kids just don't like mascots.

While working in the suit, pace yourself. Don't give it all you've got in the first ten minutes, and then slog through the next twenty until your break. Be energetic, but steady. Avoid climbing up or jumping from fixtures, stairs, benches or other items. Unless you've specifically trained beforehand to do an arranged stunt, don't attempt to improvise one with your surroundings. Not only are you putting the integrity of the costume at risk, but you're putting your own health in danger. It's extremely easy to twist or break an ankle in a mascot suit. You may also end up damaging property that your boss isn't going to enjoy paying to repair.

After The Gig

Be sure to stick to the golden rule and never let anyone see you remove your head or other pieces of your costume. Find your safe area and change quickly. Take a moment to rest, towel off and cool down. Be sure to keep drinking water. When you're ready, get your spray bottle of vodka out of your gear.

Spray bottles of vodka are the industry standard for cleaning costumes which cannot be machine-washed. Any wardrobe manager from the theater will tell you that spraying down the insides of sweaty costumes with vodka after a performance will kill bacteria which feed on the oils in our sweat, causing the rancid gym-sock smell we all hate. When the vodka dries, it takes away that smell and the bacteria that cause it. As a costume director for many venues, I use it constantly. Go for the cheapest bottle of vodka at the store, because drinkability doesn't affect how it cleans. Put it in a small, portable spray bottle and give the inside of your suit and mascot head a good once-over as soon as you get out of it. That'll give you a head start on killing any bacteria that have already decided to try and make your suit smell like feet. Your boss will also appreciate your efforts. Just be sure to clear it with them beforehand, in case the suit has a special material in it that they don't want exposed to the vodka spray. It doesn't stain and shouldn't affect most fabrics and foams, but it pays to ask beforehand and test a small area anyway.

If you have to leave immediately, just dust the insides with the spray and bag everything up. You should have a large bag or duffel to place costume items in, one that obscures what they are from the public's eye.

Once back at the Hub, be sure to spread out the costume and give it a more thorough spraying with the vodka, then let it air-dry overnight. Turn the mascot head upside down or on its side, so it can air more easily. Turn socks, feet, gloves or paws inside out and spray them, or spray inside and prop them open on the inside by sticking an empty toilet paper cardboard roll or a propped up popsicle stick inside of each. If there are any removable pads or pieces which can be hand or machine-washed, remove and launder them as soon as possible.

You will need to get some things professionally dry-cleaned eventually, but this is a great method to extend the time between trips to the cleaners and will save you a lot of money and effort in the long run.

Mascot work is much more physically demanding than for any other character, but it's a great fit for those who have a natural talent for physical expression and pantomime.

The Party Princess Handbook

Chapter Seven: Large Events

I hate parties. I really don't like public events. I hate dressing up. I'm the worst celebrity ever!
                                        Stockard Channing

Character performers are often employed for much bigger venues than just kids' parties. Many hospitals, charities, corporations and communities invite characters as a fun addition to their events. In this chapter, we'll look at some of the different kinds of large events you can expect to work.

Meet and Greets

A "meet and greet" is exactly what it sounds like. At a large event, where the focus of your interaction is not based on a birthday, an activity or a specific person, you are expected to meet most of the guests and greet them. This can mean one of two things: either you have a set-up area where you sit and people come to you (think Santa Claus on his chair in malls), or you will be working a circulating gig, where most of your time will be expended in constantly walking back and forth among the crowd, seeking out people to greet.

With a stationary meet and greet, most of the work is done for you. A handler or "greeter" will control the crowd, creating a line of people to come up to you one at a time, so they can talk with you, get pictures together, etc. With a circulating gig, you have to make an extra effort to personally approach and greet everyone you can, not just wander aimlessly through the crowd or stand in one place, waiting for the people to come to you.

101

A good circulating character will speak to or interact with everyone and especially try to provide a personal greeting to all the children at the event, as well as stop for/encourage pictures with the kids. This involves a lot of people skills and the confidence to get the attention of people in the crowd, especially if the event is small or the people reluctant to approach you.

There are pros and cons to each kind of event: sitting on a chair in the corner can get pretty dull and you may not have a chance to sneak off for a bathroom break, something that you will almost certainly need at these longer events. On the other hand, your feet will start to tire on your twentieth lap of the ballroom or conference hall while you're circulating and you may quickly feel like you're running out of new people to greet, or things to look interested in. But overall, I prefer these kinds of events to smaller parties, as the work is easier (no games, no crafts, little dancing) and it's a good time to practice my improv skills.

Shy people have a harder time with these events, especially because there is no set action script for them to memorize. I've often had younger character performers with me at meet and greets, and I have to push them to greet everyone, to take the initiative in talking about the present activities and generally just make an effort to engage. Less experienced performers may want to stay quiet and tag along behind the veterans, waiting for a cue to do something specific. It's vital that you develop your improv game early on, so you can avoid this mistake and instead be proactive, finding things to talk about at any event, in any situation, and using them to engage the guests.

Even if it's just a comment about a child's cool shirt, or hat, or asking if they've seen some fairy tale friend of yours recently – anything to draw out responses and determine which guests want to be engaged and which ones want to be left alone for the moment. You can then know whether to circle back and try again later on the shy kids, as well as learn a few names to later re-greet other children with, which always pleases both them and the parents. Everyone likes to be remembered, and the kids are usually very happy to know that they're first-name friends with their favorite character now.

Above all, it's important to remember that while you're at a meet and greet, you can never be idle, but must always be doing something, or at least develop the skills to *look* like you're always doing something.

One fun game I was playing recently with my friend Princess Rebecca was what I call the Point at Nothing, Wave to No One game. We were walking around the ice of a local skating rink during a children's skating night, greeting all the skaters on the ice. Since you can only do so many laps of a rink before you've greeted absolutely everyone, I turned and said to Rebecca under my breath, "Hey, let's play Point at Nothing, Wave to No One!"

We both took turns pointing at nothing in bemusement on the other side of the rink, as if someone far away from us had waved. We then waved enthusiastically back at the imaginary person. Imagine people on a parade float pointing out to the crowd and waving, as if singling out a specific person to say hello. We'd have a nonsensical running commentary to each other that no one else could hear over the loud music of the ice rink:

"Look over there, princess! That man has a giant sombrero! Let's point at him! Yes, and there's another gentleman, let's wave to him! My, doesn't his elephant look upset! Oh dear, is that a T-rex? I think he needs a wave too! Hello, Mr. Dinosaur! I'm sorry your arms are so short! Would you like a sandwich?"

To all the people watching us, it seemed like we were just engaged in princess chatter and waving to the skaters. To the owners of the rink, it looked like we were specifically greeting certain guests and earning our pay as entertainers. It's a lot of silly fun and it makes us look like we're doing our jobs, even if we've run out of people to greet. Plus when the guests glance over at us, we seem to be actively having fun and engaging the crowd, which makes us look more approachable.

Hospitals

Hospital visits, which are extremely common for character performers, must be treated with the utmost care. Because a patient's health is at stake, as well as their personal privacy, we must go about hospital visits in a slightly different manner than most other events.

For starters, you *cannot be sick*. It can't be stressed enough that hospitals are no place to bring a cold or a lingering cough. What might be a mild irritation to you could be horribly infectious to a patient, especially a small patient with a weakened immune system. Beside it just being common sense, hospitals almost always have rules forbidding entertainers from coming in if they have even a hint of illness. I've had to back out of more than one hospital event because I was sick, not too sick to do the job, but sick enough that it might spread. It was a disappointment to me, but the patients *always* come first. You can't justify walking into a cancer ward with a cold, just because you spent all night redoing your costume and really want to get some use out of it. Stay home and let your boss know if you're sick. They'll understand.

If you're in good condition and can attend the visit, there's still a lot you need to do to protect the patients from any outside contaminants you may bring with you. Hospital wards have hand sanitizer stations every few feet, which you'll have to use between every visit to a patient's room. Some patients will be in ISO, or isolation, so you will only be able to greet them from the door, without stepping into the room or getting close enough to touch them. Some may not even be able to have their room door opened, so you will have to wave through the window. These precautions are all very necessary, to insure the health of the patients.

When visiting a hospital, you should also remember to be quieter and less obtrusive as your character. Bigger than life is great for noisy birthday parties, but where sleeping and sick patients are concerned, maintaining a low profile is best. Even if the patients are awake, they are often tired, in pain or easily startled or upset, especially the children. It's important to greet them quietly and not upset them. Many performers doing a hospital visit for the first time feel disappointed that the child patients don't seem to be nearly as happy to see them as other kids are. It's true that patient reactions to characters may seem distant, noncommittal or uninterested. But the truth is that a lot of the patients are highly medicated and unable to fully comprehend who you are or why you're there. Even if they're alert, they may not be in the mood at that particular moment to meet a character, because they're in pain, or just coming from a treatment, or upset from long days away from their home.

There are certain things you must avoid talking about to the children, which hospitals will sometimes advise you on. "I hope you feel better soon!" is something we all naturally want to say when we see a sick person, but it's not appropriate to say to the children at the hospital. They don't want to be reminded that they're sick, and their recovery depends on keeping them in a good and cooperative mood, not depressing them. Asking them when they're going home, if they've seen their families recently, and other sensitive questions are also off-limits. Inquiring to the child about other children you may have met on a previous visit is a big taboo. If you don't see that child in the ward the second time you visit, they may have recovered and left, or they may have transferred to another hospital. Worst of all, they may have passed away. Don't bring it up.

Most importantly, if a child asks a fairy princess to use her magic to make him better, we cannot promise it. We can only tell him that he should listen to his doctor and cooperate with the nurses, because that's the best way to get better. Don't make false promises or tell the child that they'll get better very soon. Don't touch on their illness at all, and change the subject to something happier if it comes up. This is how the hospitals prefer you do things and we have to respect their wishes, even if you feel like it might temporarily cheer up the patient.

Just remember that the patients *do* appreciate your visit, very much so. Doctors and nurses will often tell us that the kids who don't respond in person to our visit will later talk about it excitedly to their families. It may not always be apparent, but your visit matters an awful lot to all the children in the hospital and their families are very grateful that your company took the time to come by.

Town Functions

Your town may have a budget that includes funding for public entertainment, like library functions or parades. Characters make a great addition to these kinds of events and if you're well-known in the community, you can expect an invite. If you're not, it never hurts to pop by your local library or town hall and drop off some business cards!

These events are much like most circulating meet and greets and have the bonus of being an amazing source of free advertisement for your company. Don't forget to load up on lots of fliers and business cards for accompanying hosts to hand out to the public, and be sure an assistant gets a ton of pictures for your website and other social media. Photos of you at town-funded functions will be a big boost to your company's reputation.

Chapter 8: Problem Customers

Your most unhappy customers are your greatest source of learning.

Bill Gates

A lot of people outside this industry seem to think that the kids are the worst part of it. Screaming kids, crying kids, hyperactive kids. When you say "problem clients," people immediately think of the children. But what we mostly mean by that is the adults.

If you're at a party and are having issues with the adults, you have two choices. You can deal with it yourself or let your hostess deal. The second one is vastly preferable, because it takes the "bad cop" role off your shoulders, so you can concentrate fully on just making the kids happy. You also won't have to leave the room for a discussion with the parent or have awkward conversations in front of the kids.

The Hostess Drives the Blocker Car

If you have a hostess with you, all questions from parents should be directed at her, period. If the parent tries to argue with you about something, sweetly smile and ask them to ask "your friend," the hostess. The hostess is the buffer between you and the client. They drive the blocker car that keeps the heat off you, so you can focus on your task at hand.

If you're the host or hostess, you will face a few different scenarios. One may be an argument over how much is owed at the end of a party. If your boss has good contracts and follow-up, this should never be in question. But some parents may try to shortchange you by saying they were quoted a different number. Always arrive at the party with a copy of the contract in hand and the actual number in mind and review it with the client *before* the party starts. Let them know that they needn't pay until the end of the party, but that you just want to confirm the number with them. If they persist in refusing to pay, you can offer to call your boss on your phone, saying you cannot do a party for less than the full payment. If they refuse to talk to the boss, then you've done all you can and must turn the issue over to the boss, saying that he or she will contact them about it later. Let your boss know by text and tell the client you must exit the party.

I don't think it's ever come down to me having to wreck a child's party due to non-payment, and I think deep down I know that I would do that party regardless, rather than disappoint a kid. But the simple threat of leaving will often get them to pay up what they owe.

If a parent insists on interfering or trying to run the character's routine themselves, as some control-freak parents will, step in and take them to one side, explaining that the character has many fun activities planned that are all carefully put together, to ensure that the birthday child will have the best day of his or her life. To avoid this problem, meet with the parent minutes before the party and ask them if they have any specific activities that they really want to see happen at the party, then convey this information to the character before they enter.

Sometimes, and I hate to say it, parents will get drunk. A lot of parents treat these parties as a social event and will take the opportunity to have a few glasses of wine with friends. If an adult is behaving inappropriately or interfering with the performance because of inebriation, kindly pull them aside and ask that they "give the performer plenty of room to work their magic." If they are being too loud or distracting, ask the group of parents to please move back or adjourn to another room so all the children can hear the performer.

If an adult or teenager is hitting on, harassing or otherwise bothering the performer, address them and lead them away immediately. Do not sugar-coat it, but instead tell them directly that the performer does not welcome harassment and that you have a firm policy about that, because some of your performers are underage. This last part is a good jab to stick in, to put the fear of legal reprisal in them. If they don't apologize, but insist they weren't doing anything wrong, keep an eye on them and do not let them approach the performer again. Complain to the client if they do. Performers have the right to feel safe at all times.

If your client promised to supply a table or space for crafts and then does not, you may have to work on the floor. But first be insistent on asking if there is any table space at all for the crafts to be done.

The host always receives payment at the end, not the performer. If the client keeps trying to insist on handing money or tips to the performer, pull them aside and explain that you take it, so as not to ruin the magic for the kids.

Dealing with Solo Party Problems

If you have the bad luck to be solo when a party problem arises, you may have to try and use the above host techniques, while still staying in character. It can be difficult to distract children enough that you can pull away for a few seconds to deal with a problematic adult, but it can be done. Whenever you need a moment, yell, "All right, let's all have a group hug around the birthday girl/boy!" and let the kids swarm the birthday child, while you dash over to deal with the situation.

109

If a client tries to pay you in front of the child, interrupt them and take their hand as if you want to hold hands with them (while obscuring the money they're offering you) and say, "OK, this was the best party ever! Would you like to show me the way outside? We can take a walk!" Lead the client by the hand outdoors, apologize and explain that you can't accept money in front of kids because it will break the illusion.

If the client argues over payment, defer to your boss. You likely won't have the contract on you, and you definitely don't have time to stick around after a party while the client argues on the phone with your boss. So accept what they are offering and tell them that while you aren't in charge of booking fees, you will definitely have your boss call them very soon about the situation. Smile and depart without further argument. They will sometimes pay up just because they don't want to dodge phone calls from your boss for the rest of the week.

If a client wants you to stay longer at a party and offers to pay more, tell them that you really can't, because you have another appointment soon. Even if you don't, your boss may not like you making deals with the client and you have no way of knowing how much extra to charge them.

It's not hard to get around most problems, which are often the result of misunderstandings. Never jump to conclusions and always be polite as pie to the client, no matter how horribly they're acting. Online reviews are a major staple of our reputation and you don't want to earn a spiteful Yelp revenge-post because you got the deposit amount wrong. But be just as firm when you know you're in the right and don't give in to bullying. Your best way to avoid any problems is to always go over routines, payment and other issues upfront, before the party. If you can't get a host to do it, call the parents ten minutes before you enter as a performer and give them a "friendly checking-in" to confirm everything first.

Chapter 9: Legal Issues

Compromise is the best and cheapest lawyer.

Robert Louis Stevenson

Copyrights, trademarks . . . how to walk the line and not do the time? It's an inevitable fact that some of the characters your company uses will undoubtedly be generic versions of popular media characters. It's just what kids want to see and even though we'd like it to be any other way, the market demands it. You have to learn to err on the side of caution and respect when making and performing a generic character, as well as not infringing on copyrights in your marketing and advertising.

What is Copyright, What is Trademark, What is a Patent?

Copyright means that a company has legally claimed an intellectual or creative property as their own, either because they created it or bought the creative rights to it from another company. They own that thing entirely, because they thought it up or bought it from the person who did. This usually applies to creative works like films, books, plays, video games, music, etc. Trademark, on the other hand, is not necessarily something a company invented, but because it's so closely associated with their company, it's reasonable to assume that if another company in the industry used it, the two would get mixed up. This applies to names of things, like Apple Computers, Pepsi soda and Kodak film. A patent is granted to people who wish to retain exclusive intellectual and manufacturing rights for technical items like inventions, which they have proven they were the first to design.

For example, Apple has a trademark on the name iPhone, because they invented it. They have also have a trademark on the word "apple," because it's associated with their product. Another computer company cannot call anything it sells "apple," because someone could easily get mixed up and think they were buying real Apple electronics. But another company that is NOT a computer company can call something Apple. . . Apple socks, Apple purse, Apple sandwich . . . because no one is going to mix up a genuine Apple computer with an Apple pair of socks.

Disney has a copyright on the name Mickey Mouse, because they invented it and as a cartoon, it's a creative property. And considering how much merchandise Mickey can fit on, no one else is allowed to use this name, not even socks or purses or sandwiches, because it would be too easy to trick buyers into thinking they were buying real Mickey Mouse merchandise.

Disney has a trademark on the image of Princess Ariel from their Little Mermaid franchise, because they invented how she looks. You can get around that by designing your own mermaid character who does not look a lot like Ariel, but you cannot use the name Ariel itself for that character. They also have a trademark on her name, when used in conjunction with mermaid characters, because even though they didn't invent the name Ariel, they were the first to commercially use it for a mermaid character. You can call your t-shirt store Ariel's Shirt Store and sell golf shirts, but if you call it that and then sell nothing but mermaid shirts and mermaid memorabilia, you may be violating their trademark. Trademark is all about making sure other companies can't take your name that you built a reputation and following on, and throw it onto their stuff to confuse people. You wouldn't want another restaurant painting their place to look like a McDonald's and then advertising that they sell Big Macs, would you? It probably wouldn't taste the same as a Big Mac at all and you'd feel tricked.

An interesting development came about in 2013, when Disney tried to trademark the name "Snow White," despite the fact that it's a public domain name, having been in fairy tales for over a hundred years and not an original invention by Disney. Disney's lawyers argued that their version of Snow White is so universally popular that everyone just automatically associates the name Snow White with Disney, and for anyone else to use the name is inviting legal confusion.

They applied for a trademark that would cover TV, film, internet, radio and theatrical displays of the character, but not books. So other people can still use the name Snow White in books, either fiction or non-fiction. This led to a great deal of confusion and rumor among character performers. I've heard everything in forums from "Disney bought the rights to Snow White" to "Disney now owns the rights to all the old fairy tale characters."

To be clear, Disney cannot "buy the rights" to something in the public domain, any more than Apple computers can buy the rights to all apples everywhere. Something in the public domain belongs to the public. And, as most argue, this trademark of theirs would really not hold up in court if they tried to use it against, say, a generic school play. It was mostly done to protect their image of *their* Snow White from being appropriated and used for media. The dress style, hair color, outfit color, etc. all mark that particular Snow White version as Disney's, and this trademark will help them better win disputes against those who try to mimic it in movies or films. But it does not mean Disney *owns* Snow White herself, or that they will be kicking down the doors of storybook publishers for including her name.

The bottom line is that copyrights and trademark disputes are tricky things, and unless you have the bottomless pockets that Disney lawyers have, you should err on the side of caution. But public domain names like Prince Charming, Cinderella, Rapunzel, Sleeping Beauty, The Snow Queen, and yes, even Snow White, should be perfectly fine to use, so long as the characters to which you affix them have been visibly differentiated from Disney's or any other company's properties.

Cease and Desist

Let's say you thought you were doing everything right at the company for which you work, legally speaking. But one day your boss gets a Cease and Desist, often just called a C&D, in the mail. A letter from a very big company is telling you that they saw a picture of one of your performers online and they think you're stepping on their trademark, either by using a trademarked name or being too close to the visual of their own characters.

First things first: don't panic. That letter may look all scary and legal and even have been sent from *a very official lawyer's office*, but the gist of any C&D is just that: cease and desist. In other words, please knock off what you're doing.

Because a lot of people don't have a firm understanding of the law, they think a C&D is a terrifying thing, especially if it includes a bunch of demands. Demands that you pay them a hefty fine, or turn over your costumes to them at once, or something equally silly.

Let's get one thing straight: a lawyer's office is not a *judge's* office. A lawyer can't make you pay a fine. Nobody can, except a judge, who is also the only one other than a police officer who can legally *issue* you a fine. A lawyer can't confiscate your costumes, only a judge can order that to be done. And even then, that can happen only *after* a trial finding you guilty of some wrongdoing. And even *then*, only if they determine that you're the kind of person who would otherwise continue to use your costumes to violate copyright, or do some other illegal mischief with them.

Lawyers are not the police, and they know it. But they also know that small businesses are easy to frighten with empty threats. Letters demanding money and actions in very angry-sounding legalese are totally meaningless, but very effective at scaring companies into halting whatever behavior was angering the lawyers in the first place. I have seen C&Ds that demand a thousand dollars in fines and for the party company in question to turn over all of their costumes at once. Not one word of that is enforceable and you're only lining the lawyer's pockets if you're fool enough to pay them what they demand.

By definition, a Cease and Desist from a lawyer is a request that you immediately stop doing whatever it is you're doing that they don't like, or else they may take legal action against you. Anyone can send a cease and desist letter, even you! But they mostly come from lawyers, on behalf of another person or company who has asked the lawyer to send it.

Let's say you're using pictures of Mickey Mouse on your company website, for example, and Disney sends you a letter, via their lawyers, telling you to stop and that you owe them $500 in fines. It's not a judge's order, a legal summons, or a court injunction. It has even less authority than a parking ticket. You do not have to pay that $500, and frankly you'd be silly to even consider doing so. The only thing you should do is take those trademarked images down at once and apologize in a return letter.

If you violate the C&D by continuing to use the Mickey Mouse images on your site, Disney can then go to a judge and say, "Look, we asked them to stop, but they didn't. We want to take them to court now to make them stop." The judge will then decide if this case has enough merit to warrant a trial.

If a *judge* issues you a cease and desist on behalf of the other company, then you must stop what you're doing and the court has the right to fine you if you don't follow it. If you take down your pictures of Mickey Mouse on your website, but then put them up again a year later, you may be slapped with a fine by the court and forced to pay it.

Some character companies erroneously think that Disney or other large companies can "shut down" a party company with a C&D. Well, technically they can ask *you* to shut your company down, but they can't force you to shut down, any more than they can force you to change your name to Jasper P. Shenanigans. But they *can* take you to court and get your company shut down by a judge, which is not something you want to go through. In this extreme case, your best bet is to simply write back apologizing for infringement, say that you didn't realize it was that much of a problem and that you will remove the offending material and redesign the offending costumes to be more generic. This is usually a satisfactory response for them. You'd really have to go off the deep end on trademarked material to get on their radar so much that they want to shut down your whole business, so just play it safe in the first place and this won't happen.

Some trademark holders are more persistent than others. When the show "Barney and Friends" first came out, the owners of that property were unrelenting in tracking down and suing character companies for having mascot suits even close to Barney. This is a little more understandable, as Barney is essentially *just* a mascot suit and making one identical to him for your own company is way over the line. Any parent would mistake a well-made knockoff Barney suit for the real thing. But the owners of Barney had a reputation for being threat-happy about anything related to their character. They even went on legal rampages against anyone online who dared to insult the purple dinosaur. Of course, this was back in the early days of the internet, when people undoubtedly though they could control and censor it like printed media (a laughable idea now).

Barney's legal witch-hunt against lookalike characters has since died down, now that the show is no longer produced and its popularity has diminished. But it shows that some companies are way more aggressive about their trademarks than others and you need to keep abreast of who is all right with generics and who is not.

Another thing to consider is location. The closer you are to a performance venue that is the inspiration for your generics, the more trouble you may court. A Disney-lookalike Cinderella in Ohio is not going to have the same problems that a lookalike Cinderella standing outside Disney World will have. Understand that if your characters appear close to where the official characters are meant to be seen, you run the risk of being mistaken for their own employees. And nothing's more humiliating to a company than photos of some party princess drinking in a bar or smoking in front of the Magic Kingdom parking lot. Photos of it will spread, tweets will fly and absolutely no one will stop to think that she *doesn't* work for the Disney parks, even after an explanation. All anyone will remember is the picture and it will be very damaging to the company's reputation. They can't control what your own employees do, so they'd rather not get you mixed up with *their* employees. So keep geography in mind when you do generics.

It's a fact that as the party character industry grows exponentially, it becomes harder and harder for large media companies to turn a blind eye to us. They need to protect their image and not be saddled with negative publicity that's created by people over whom they have absolutely no control. So stay on the side of generic, public-domain characters as much as possible and respect the trademarks of others.

A simple way to make your Brand X character more distinct is to change the hair style, alter the cut of the costume, add short sleeves or long, make it a slightly different color shade, include different accessories and give it a distinctly different name. Avoid talking about trademarked characters at parties. If a child asks you how so-and-so Disney character is doing, answer with, "All my friends are having a great time today!" or other vague response. The kids can use the names, but you cannot.

When doing public events, make sure the event coordinator knows to use *your* generic character names on fliers, ads, websites, etc., as well to use photos of you and not Trademarked clip art or images grabbed online. Many people still have this idea that we have "licenses" to do what we do for our companies and that we can use whatever names and images we want. Make sure they understand the difference and supply them with printed material or pre-made digital ads to use for their events.

Stay on the right side of the law and you won't have any problematic letters in your mailbox!

Chapter 10: Promotion and Making the Most of Social Media

Money coming in says I've made the right marketing decisions.
Adam Osborne

Active, endless promotion is vitally important to character companies. Rarely do we have a brick-and-mortar store where clients will happen to walk by and notice our business. Added to which, many consumers still aren't even aware that we *are* a business, thinking that we must work for a theater, or are the employees of whatever event location is hosting us at a gig.

Social media is one of the most important tools that small businesses have at their disposal. Although the bulk of character company business still comes from word of mouth, we are increasingly seeing a surge in online research by busy parents who want to find the closest and highest-quality party company that will fit within their budget.

In addition to a well-designed and constantly updated website, it's practically essential for companies to have their own Facebook page now. Running promotions, advertising sales and promoting different booking packages is easier than ever, thanks to Facebook's call-to-action and discount button options. More importantly, the modern customer expects a Facebook page for practically every established business, in order to read feedback from customers and get the latest news.

If you're not the owner of the business, you might think that your responsibilities towards marketing and advertisement are few and far between. However, a good character company relies on its employees to help grow the brand, by handing out business cards whenever possible, talking up the business in their own community and really functioning as "brand ambassadors" for their specific company.

I always know a performer works for a good company if that performer has a stack of related business cards on their person at all times. The most successful companies instill a feeling of shared responsibility for advertising with all of their performers.

This isn't done to unload work off the boss and onto the employees, but rather to bring in business that will benefit everyone. You may think that if you work a retail job and you're not expected to go talk up your retail job at every moment and hand out business cards, then why do it for a character company? It's necessary because character companies are smaller, almost entirely family-owned and really need the extra help. Plus, a retail job pays you per hour for your shift, no matter what. But if a character company doesn't get as much work, then that means fewer bookings and less paying work for *you*. So it's in your best interests as a performer to always be committed to steering potential clients towards your company!

Added to this, *you* are the face of your company as a performer. When clients book the company, they're booking you and your fellow workers. Selling yourself sells the company and translates to a bigger personal following for you as an individual performer, meaning more requests for you at bookings and more steady work overall.

I always have a stack of business cards for the companies I work with and I hand them out with my name written on the back of each card and an invitation for the client to mention me at booking, so that my boss knows who made the referral.

When going around my community, I'll introduce myself at local places like libraries, rec centers, party stores and children's play destinations. I'll tell the managers a little about the company I work for and ask if I can leave a few cards for parents to take. People are almost always happy to oblige and I've gotten bookings more than once from a curious parent who picked up a business card left by the register at a store. They may let you hang small fliers if they have a corkboard nearby for community items. The post office also usually has a small place for community announcements or fliers and you should definitely ask to place a little advertisement there.

It's surprising just how many places would like to use your services, but don't even know you exist. Library networks, gym networks with daycare services like the YMCA, and Boys and Girls Clubs especially need to be informed of what you offer. Sending them a little introductory packet, plus a small coupon for their first booking, can't hurt at all. Better yet, go in person with a manila envelope full of info about your work, your price list, a letter of introduction from your boss and some colorful pictures of the characters you offer.

It may be a little daunting to walk into a cold-call at one of these places and offer an information packet, but did you know there's one surefire way to always get their attention and *never* be turned away before you make your pitch?

Show up in costume.

It's the easiest thing in the world, really! Buy a cheap balloon on a string from the grocery store or nearby party place, which will cost you maybe three dollars. Get dolled up in your cutest work costume and walk into the location you want to pitch to, carrying the balloon. *No one* will turn you away. They'll definitely smile and laugh, but they won't be annoyed with you. It's always amusing when something like that happens and they may think it's someone's birthday at the office, or that you were hired for a telegram. Even when they find out you're just there to present some information, they'll still be amused and won't send you packing. Leave the information packet and balloon with the front desk, along with your card to give you a call.

Just be sure you have the balloon. I'm not sure why it works better with a balloon, but it always does. I think it's the law of reciprocation: you gave them a balloon, so now they feel obligated to give you a call. Either way, three dollars is a good investment to get a couple hundred dollars' worth of bookings from them!

Remember that you should always be looking for new and creative ways to help advertise for your company. Talk up your company to your relatives and friends with kids, mention it to teachers and others who work with children and volunteer for your boss every so often to do free community events where you can hand out fliers. Every little bit of effort will translate into much bigger sales!

As for how you present yourself on your own social media sites, well, this is a problem that's continuously popping up in the news. Employees of any kind of business seem to be forever embarrassing themselves and their parent companies by proxy through some kind of social media site, be it Twitter, Facebook, Instagram or a number of other places. One badly-worded tweet or out-of-context photo can go viral and end up costing you your job, as well as your employer their carefully curated online image.

Have a little common sense when you work for a company. Post all the silly pictures you want, but set them to private, so only you and friends can see them. Always stop and think of how an image you post may reflect on your company, before you post it. Never post inappropriate public photos of you in costume and acting out of character, because a future customer is bound to find them. And do not tie your social media sites to your business' site. One of the reasons my companies use names like Princess Marty and Princess Delia and Princess Ashley is to keep the actors' personal lives separate from the public business pages. If you have a personal site or online information that you feel might reflect badly when viewed by a client, (say, you also work with a burlesque troupe and there are racy photos of you somewhere online), then use a character name and create a separate social media account for it. Strictly separate your personal photos from your work photos and don't mix them between accounts. Only tag something with your company's name, or your personal name, if you're sure that following that tag won't lead a client into viewing content you don't want them to see!

Remember that an ounce of prevention is worth a pound of cure. In other words, it's easy to take precautions, but really hard to fix problems!

SECTION THREE: RESOURCES & MAINTENANCE

Although this handbook is primarily for character performers and not owners of party companies, it's important to include a section on company resources in order to familiarize new performers with how the company works and what to look for when trying to find a good company to hire you.

There's also a growing trend of character performers maintaining their own supplies and costumes, separate from their employer's stock. I have an arrangement with my bosses wherein I use my own costumes and props, never theirs. I prefer it this way, because the costumes are tailored to my measurements and I never have to worry that someone else has perspired in them, or torn or dirtied them. It also saves me time and mileage if I can go straight from my house to a gig, without stopping at the Hub to change. Although it's more expensive for me to buy and make my own costumes, it's worth it to me in the long run. You may find this arrangement works well for you too!

The Party Princess Handbook

Chapter 11: Buying Costumes

If human beings had genuine courage, they'd wear their costumes every day, not just on Halloween.

Douglas Coupland

Costumes are the most important investment for any party company. It's not an exaggeration to say that the quality of your costume will make or break your performance, especially since most parents judge performers by their costume first and their acting second (children tend to do it the other way around, but they're not the ones paying you). A bad performer may squeak by in reviews if she has an amazing costume, but a terrific performer will always be perceived as much worse if her costume is poor in quality.

Nowadays, there are more costumes resources than ever for party companies, so there's no excuse for trying to do your work in a cheap Halloween costume. Although it may seem expensive to pay out $300 for a princess dress, a little math tells us that the costume will pay for itself in just six parties, or fewer if you get good tips.

Buying Online

There are hundreds of online seamstresses and companies that take custom work from the character performer trade and they're easy to dig up with just a little searching. One good place to find them is on Etsy, where you can get handmade costumes in your size for very reasonable prices.

127

If you have enough time to wait for shipping, there are some quite nice costumes from China and other places overseas that can be found on Etsy and eBay. It's important to read the reviews first before buying and not jump at the cheapest price, but don't let the fact that it's from overseas fool you into thinking it's low quality. There are plenty of foreign sellers who have great starter costumes. They won't be jaw-droppingly perfect, but they'll be more than good enough for you to start your costume collection. If you sew or a friend can sew, you might even touch these basic costumes up to make them better!

The important thing to look for when buying is quality and durability. A pretty costume may look significantly more high-quality in photos than it does when you actually receive it, and there's no way to tell from a picture if cheap, thin material was used to make it. So do your homework and read customer reviews before buying!

A Few Things to Avoid When Buying:

- ✓ Costumes with velcro closures (they stick to everything in your costume wardrobe, tear delicate fabrics and attract wig hair)
- ✓ Side zippers on dresses (not easy to get into or out of)
- ✓ Costumes claiming to fit a wide range of sizes (S through L, for example, we call these "one size fits none")
- ✓ Costumes without a clear size measurement chart for reference (a Korean medium might be an American extra small)
- ✓ Boot covers for shoes (just spring for full boots. Covers never look nice, no matter how they may look in a seller's pictures)

Buying Wigs

One of the biggest mistakes new performers make is in trying to economize on wigs, whether by using or dyeing their own hair, or by buying inferior wigs. Using your own hair instead of a wig is a hotly-contested choice among performers, especially women. It can go well, or it can look very bad. I prefer wigs simply because they cut down in prep time before parties and they have that "bigness" that visually balances out the rest of your costume, so your head doesn't look small in comparison to your outfit. It also allows you to swap characters with a stand-in who may not have the same hair as you. But it's ultimately up to you.

I did an informal poll with some performers who had been a year out from their first parties and they all unanimously encouraged investing in quality wigs. New people may not understand the difference between a good wig and a bad one, or think that you must opt for expensive human hair ones. A good synthetic wig will not frizz, tangle or have a plastic-y, fake sheen to it. It will also not shed lots of hair and go thin quickly. It will feel like real hair and have a fully adjustable inside band to fit most heads.

I do not recommend human hair wigs for any character, because they are too expensive to keep buying replacements, far too fragile to take a constant beating and they break down more quickly, due to split ends and other damage that synthetic wigs don't see.

A good synthetic wig is likely not going to be the one you find at the party store, or on eBay from China for $12, no matter how nice it looks in photos. But it also doesn't have to be the $300 affair you see listed in a private Etsy shop. Generally speaking, I look to invest $50-$75 per wig, unless it's a very long, complicated one for a character like Rapunzel. The price I pay without styling. I did spend $100 on my original Cinderella twist updo, from a drag store on eBay, but now I do my own styling and save a lot of money because of that. I also try to buy in person, which is where local wig shops come in handy. They don't have a large variety of colors, but their wigs are often very high quality, reasonably priced and sometimes on sale or clearance. Best of all, you can examine them in person and see if the thickness and texture are to your liking.

These shops also carry all the styling supplies you will need.

As always, I recommend Youtube video tutorials for styling your own wigs, as a free and fast educational source. It's not nearly as difficult as people assume and you will pocket up to $150 in savings if you style your own.

Making Your Own Costumes

If you know how to sew or have a friend or relative who does, you can easily make your own costumes. Practically every costume you want has a generic counterpart in the Simplicity, McCalls and Butterick pattern catalogs at your local sewing store, or you can buy them online, direct from the pattern company. Pattern-makers pride themselves on sensing costuming trends that are dictated by popular characters in media, so you'd hard-pressed not to find what you're looking for. If you need a generic version of some movie or show character, there's a good pattern out there for you that's in the beginner to intermediate skill range. Making your own costumes will save you tons of money. A custom dress that may cost $500 on Etsy will only cost you about $80 in materials, plus your labor time of a few days. It's just a smart investment to learn how to sew.

Your local JoAnn and other craft stores have ongoing sewing classes that are an inexpensive and easy way to learn how to sew. I'm self-taught in sewing, and I can assure you it's not nearly as hard as it seems. It's actually quite fun to learn! You can learn how to do simple repairs on costumes in just one day.

A great free source of endless sewing lessons is on Youtube (is there anything that site *can't* teach us how to do?). Anything you want to learn, there's a video that will teach you how to do it, quickly and easily.

As I mentioned before, you can also buy a cheaper costume and dress it up to make it more original and fancy. There's nothing I can't make better with a packet of craft store rhinestones and a tube of E6000 glue, or some lace appliques and an iron. You can also do simple sleeve and skirt alterations on a base costume, which is much easier than designing from scratch.

Renting Costumes

Many people who don't work in this industry erroneously believe we rent outfits from costume rental shops. This is a crazy notion, as that would get incredibly expensive after only a few rentals, plus we'd have to pay the shop every time a kid got something on the costume. The only exception to this rule is mascot costumes, as it's sometimes cheaper to rent than to buy. However, rental shops *are* a great resource for buying old costumes that you can fix up. If you can find a shop that's clearing out its stock, you may get some great costumes and props at a bargain!

The Party Princess Handbook

Chapter 12: Maintenance and Storing

The more storage you have, the more stuff you accumulate.
Alexis Stewart

A good costume company will have a separate room at their Hub for storage and changing. But if you keep your own stock of costumes, it can be a little harder to find the space. Not everyone has a spare room in their house that they can dedicate just to costume storage! However, it's not hard to find a spot for your character items, if you give it a little thought and pick out a good corner to dedicate as a storage area. The size of the area doesn't matter, as long as you know how to organize it properly. Maintenance is also key, if you want your costumes to stay looking as good as the day you bought them.

Storage

The one thing to remember is that costumes must be stored carefully, to avoid damage, lasting wrinkles or stretching. Hanging a costume improperly can stretch the shoulders of it out of shape, so that it doesn't sit well on the performer. It also creates wrinkles, which adds unnecessary work to your morning prep if you have to haul out the iron and smooth them. Storing wigs flat on a shelf instead of on foam heads can ruin their styling and put folds in the inner caps, as well as flatten out fibers on one side. So be sure your storage setup at home is protecting your investments, not hurting them.

All costumes should be hung on appropriate hangers (trouser clips for pants, cushioned or dress hangers for dresses, etc.) and should be hung correctly. A skirt should be hung by the waistband from a trouser clip hanger, not folded in half and stuffed into a regular shirt hanger. Good dresses will have little ribbon loops inside the bodice that attach to the tiny hooks on plastic hangers, so that the dress itself doesn't rest on the hanger and stretch. If you make your costumes yourself, or own costumes that don't have these loops, be sure to add them in. It only takes some cheap dollar ribbon and a few minutes with a needle and thread. If a costume is too heavy and bends wire and plastic hangers, get some quality wooden hangers instead.

Shoes should be placed in a hanging shoe pocket, so that you always know where a pair is and don't lose one. Boots should go flat on the floor. If you don't have boot trees, keep them standing upright with a cardboard tube from a roll of paper towels.

Props like crowns, hats, gloves, jewelry and other accessories should be sorted by type and placed in little bins, either labeled or clear plastic so that the contents can be seen at a glance. Keep your items separate so you're not digging through them in a hurry before a gig, or trying to untangle a necklace clasp that's hooked onto a ballroom glove and is tearing at the fabric. The same goes for any props like storybooks, games, gemstones or coins. The easier they are to find, the more time and frustration you save.

Portable zip-up wardrobes are cheap and readily available at any chain store like Walmart or Target. For around $20, you can buy a tall, 36-inch wide wardrobe that can be stashed in any corner of your house and will hold up to a dozen sizable costumes, plus a hanging shoe organizer. Just assemble the inside metal clothes rack frame and stretch the canvas cover over it. It's usually waterproof and unzips in the front for easy costume access. Since I have two cats, I really love my wardrobe's ability to keep out stray cat hair and furry friends who may want to try and sleep on my costumes.

For wigs, a few basic wall shelves from IKEA (I like the flat black Ekby shelves and matching brackets) will run you maybe ten dollars per shelf and will hold between three and five wigs on foam heads, depending on the size of shelf you buy. They can be installed on any wall in minutes and are very sturdy. Best of all, you can stack them in a set of three and have more than enough room to keep all your wigs nice, while freeing up bookcase or table space.

Designate a spot for your costume storage that will be only for that use, even if it's just a small corner of one room. Try to make it a habit never to let your costume pieces or props spread out around your house. It's tempting to drag yourself home after a long work day and dump your costume on the bedroom floor, before taking a nap or a shower. I used to toss my crown onto a hat hook by my front door every time I came inside. But this makes it harder for you to track down the pieces you need when you *really* need them, right before an event. Keeping them in one spot every single day will ensure that you can always find them.

Storing Difficult Items

Some items, like large props or big event pieces, may defy ordinary storage solutions. A swimming mermaid tail, for example, can be up to five feet long and three feet wide at the fluke, and *must* be stored perfectly flat, out of sunlight or heat. So you'll have to get creative with storing unusual items (my mermaid tail lies flat under my couch in the living room).

If something can be hung from a hook to keep it out of the way, drill some holes in the ceiling and twist in a few sturdy curtain hook screws, then suspend plastic hooked wires down from which to hang items. If it must be stored flat, look for unused space beneath or behind beds and sofas. Use flat garment bags to zip items into before putting them away for flat storage. And avoid storage units or basements that have no climate control or air conditioning, or you may end up with water damage, musty smell and mold on your items. If you have to use a basement, get a separate, waterproof zip-up storage wardrobe that will protect your items from humidity and water damage.

Mascot costumes can be big and cumbersome, with a large head and lots of foam padding. The head can sit on a shelf without a wig head or anything to support it, but the body should always be hung up to keep the inner padding from lying on a horizontal surface and gradually flattening out on one side.

Maintenance

Due to our job mainly involving sweating, lots of movement and poking from little kids, party costumes will start to degrade almost immediately if you don't care for them. A hundred-dollar specialized character wig will quickly turn into a lumpy, frizzy mess if you simply toss it on the shelf after every party, and a costume jacket that cost you several hundred will be rendered unusable if you let the underarms yellow.

The best way to maintain costume quality is to simply take a lot of precautions when wearing them. Always have an undershirt beneath your costume to protect it from sweat, and wear stick-on dress shields to avoid underarm sweat and discoloration. The upper back, neckline, collar and *especially* the underarms of costumes are always the first to yellow, stain and give the costume a gross, dingy appearance. And they're the one spot you often can't just cut out and replace, unlike ruffles or hems. So include a cheap bulk pack of dress shields and a few tank tops in your first line of defense against depre-ciation of your investment. At events, try to avoid items that stain, like grass (hoist long skirts up to avoid it when walking), dark beverages, face-paints and especially *green*

cake frosting. Green cake frosting is the bane of party performers everywhere. It dyes fabric the moment it touches you and
it's very hard to scrub out. Blue cake frosting is the second
worst, but other colors are a bit safer and ones like yellow or
orange in comparison are hardly a matter of concern at all.

Maintenance of your costumes is something that should be
done on a regular basis, starting with spot-cleaning them after
each gig and ending with a full dry-cleaning every few months.
In between washings, you can spray costumes down with
cheap vodka in a spray bottle, which kills odor-causing
bacteria (see Chapter Five, *Mascots* for more information on
this technique). You can also do this for the insides of wigs,
giving them a really quick dusting with the spray to kill any
bacteria lurking in the sweat from your scalp.

Costumes can rarely be shoved in a washing machine and
sent for a spin, so you must wash them by hand in a sink or
the tub. But don't just drop them bodily into a bathtub full of
water! The goal is to expose as little of the costume to soap
and water as possible. Wash only fabrics that you are sure
can be exposed to water, and wash only the parts that are
actually dirty – the torso, underarm and back areas usually
absorb a lot of sweat and discoloration, and the ends of
sleeves can get dingy. Use a very gentle detergent and avoid
dumping a lot of it in, or you'll have quite a time rinsing it all
out again. Avoid bleach or lightening agents. Always test a
small spot on the fabric first to see if it is colorfast. If it's a
dark fabric, it may bleed dark fabric dye during the first
washing or two and you don't want that to leak onto another
part of the costume!

Costume fabrics with glitter details on them will often lose
glitter in the wash, so be extra careful around them. There are
some heat-set glitter fabrics that don't shed glitter, but you
can't always tell which ones they are. If you notice that glitter
rubs off from your costume onto other things while wearing it,
then it will undoubtedly come off in water. Laundry pens and
careful spot cleaning can be used to get little stains out

without harming special fabric too much.

Hang the costume up carefully over the shower curtain rod or a folding clothes rack, to let it air-dry from both sides. Do not blow-dry or heat it, as this may warp or shrink the costume.

Any costume that comes in contact with chlorinated water (like a pool party pirate or mermaid) should have the chlorine neutralized in a bath of baking soda and lukewarm water. Chlorine will eat away at fabric and other materials until they're bleached or destroyed, so neutralize it as soon as possible.

As for wigs, they can be trickier to maintain. I always advise keeping them on foam wig stands, with a large hat pin through the top if they're heavy and won't stay on by them-selves. This makes them easier to store and style, plus it helps them keep their shape and not crease on the inside, or mat down one side of the hair. A styled wig, like a princess updo or sprayed bangs, *must* be stored on a foam head to keep its shape. Wigs shouldn't be brushed any more than they require for styling. It's actually better to brush your wig as little as you can, while still keeping it tangle-free and neat. A wide-toothed comb or specialized wig brush is a better bet than using an ordinary hair brush.

Wigs can be washed (so long as they're not pre-styled or set with hairspray) in wig shampoo that can be found online or at most wig beauty stores. If you have a badly tangled wig, try using a spray bottle that contains one-quarter unscented fabric softener, such as Downy, and three-quarters water. Shake it up and give the wig quite a few sprays. The softener will help the wig snarls slide apart as you comb them through. Patience and an hour in front of the TV with a wig head will turn a tangled mess back into a useable wig. Just don't spring for the scented fabric softener. I did that once and ended up with a Rapunzel wig that smelled strongly of floral dryer sheets.

Wig caps can usually be tossed in the washer, along with cotton gloves. Satin-finish gloves can go in the wash, but *not* the dryer, as this will ruin their shiny finish and make them fuzzy. As a rule, I just never let anything party-related go in the dryer, but instead hang it in my bathroom to dry.

Anything handmade should not be put in a washer, even if it's small and seems OK, but should instead be rinsed out in the sink. The stitching may come out from the hems otherwise, or the color may bleed. So when in doubt, just rinse it out!

As for props, they're usually pretty sturdy. Inspect all your props once a month, including storybooks, for signs of damage or wear. Replace them as necessary. The only thing you should be really be concerned about is sanitizing your props. Little kids like to put their hands in their mouths, fingers up their noses, touch everything on the ground and then touch your props while you use them. I once had a little girl sneeze right into my wishing box, covering all the gems inside with spit. Be sure to clean your props regularly, especially after any sneezing or drooling incidents. This isn't just for your own health, but the health of the next group of children you entertain as well.

Chapter 13: Skin and Hair Care

*Take good care of your skin and hydrate. If you have good skin,
everything else will fall into place.*

Liya Kebede

This book just wouldn't be complete if I didn't include a
section on one of my favorite topics: caring for your hair and
skin!

Character performers take a real beating on these two fronts.
If we're not wearing hot, scratchy wigs that wreck our natural
hair, we're caking on makeup that clogs our pores and dries
out our skin. How do you keep up with the damage that just
comes with the job?

For starters, you need to rethink your ordinary skin routine.
Just washing in the morning and at night is not going to cut
it, even if you play only male roles. Makeup is still required for
all face characters, regardless of gender. And the constant
heavy applications mean that your skin is sweating and
suffocating for several hours a week under a thick layer of
powder, paint and oils.

Make sure you have a good daily cleansing regimen already in
place and stick to it. Use non-foaming facial cleansers to avoid
dry skin and always moisturize after washing and before bed,
using an oil-free lotion specifically designed for your face. If
you suffer from acne, character makeup will only make it

worse, so see a dermatologist if you have trouble controlling breakouts. It may be a sign of hormonal imbalance that can be alleviated through medication.

It's important to always work with *clean* cosmetics, sponges and brushes. Don't hoard the same makeup supplies for years, but instead check any expiration dates and abide by them. Don't keep creams and mascaras around for more than six months. If you absolutely must share with other performers, make sure to wash brushes frequently or provide your own sponges and brushes, to avoid spreading infections or bacteria. Clean your brushes every week with a brush cleaner or some of your own antibacterial facial cleanser.

Always apply a good sunscreen before applying your makeup. I can't emphasize this enough! Daily sunscreen use is the best possible thing you can do for your skin. Not only does it make a nice smooth priming base for your makeup, it's just smart skin care. Even if it's cloudy out or you're only going to be in the car a little while, sun will still damage your skin. Remember to apply it to the backs of your hands and arms as well!

When out on the job, use oil-absorbing sheet packs to control shine on your face, instead of dabbing on more powder layers. The sheets will take away any oily spots without disturbing your makeup. Bring moistened facial wipes with you on party days and when you finish all your gigs for the day, clean your face off thoroughly with the wipes before driving home. The trick is to never let makeup sit on your face for any longer than it absolutely must. At home, do another wash of your face to remove any traces of makeup. A good way to take off mascara and eyeliner gently is with extra virgin olive oil and a Q-tip. When you're all done cleaning, apply a moisturizer.

During the week, you can do an exfoliating scrub and inexpensive clay mask to clean out your pores. You can also use an acid treatment or Vitamin C serum to help your skin get back to the ideal pH levels that help it fight off acne-causing bacteria and infection.

142

And always remember to be careful about applying spirit gum or other adhesives to your skin! Use a good gum remover, instead of just pulling the spirit gum off your face.

Mascot performers don't have to worry about makeup, but they do run the risk of breakouts and other problems caused by excessive sweating, leading to moist, damp conditions on the skin and scalp that invite infection. Always remember to wear a good absorbent sweatband to keep sweat off your face. If you find your scalp is getting too sweaty, rub a dry shampoo or a bit of cornstarch into your hair before a performance. This will absorb sweat and keep your scalp dry.

A lot of character performers worry about their skin, but not many give the same kind of consideration towards their hair. I guess that's because our faces are often the focal point of our characters, but hardly anyone ever sees our real hair while it's hidden under a wig! So a few split ends aren't a cause for concern in the way that acne or skin flakiness might be. But whether you know it or not, character performing can be pretty rough on one's mane. We spend way more time than the average person with a hot, restricting cap over our heads, made of pulling and friction-causing nylon or plastic weft ends.

If you have to spend 6-10 hours every weekend with a hot, harsh thing on your head, you will have hair problems, resulting in the following types of situations:

A wig cap, generally worn to keep your hair up and out of sight when under a wig, is made of a pantyhose-like nylon material, or a slightly gentler stretchy mesh. Both are still universally dreadful for your hair, because they're tight, they pull at your hair right around your hairline and near the roots (causing breakage and hair pulling) and they hold in moist heat to your head for several hours, which can increase bacterial and fungal levels in your scalp, which in turn can lead to dandruff, flaking, blocked hair follicles, increased oil production and even hair loss. It also rubs against the ends of your hair, which are piled inside under the cap, exacerbating split end damage.

On top of all that, you wear the actual wig, which is designed to look good on the outside, not baby your real hair on the inside. The interior of a wig is a woven mesh of lace and plastic netting, often with helpful combs and hooks that keep a heavy wig in place, but pull at your hair. Constantly wearing a wig causes "mechanical damage," i.e. rubbing and friction along the hair line, which can lead to hair loss in those areas. And it's just one more layer that's keeping your scalp from proper ventilation, holding in sweat and heat.

Another problem that's been cropping up even more lately is the issue of damage caused by lace-front wigs. Many princesses use them now for characters that have swept-back hair which must look natural at the scalp line. Lace-front wigs, even if you avoid gluing them down, cause intense mechanical damage along the hairline due to their harsh, Brillo-like "lace" liners at the front, which scrape and irritate hair follicles and can cause incredibly bad infections if misused.

So how do you keep ahead of all this damage?

First of all, ditch the pantyhose wig cap. They cause more hairline damage than a looser, open-top net cap, and they hold in heat more. A net cap is actually easier to put on, too! Just pull it over your head like a shirt, then pull it right back up by the un-elasticized band edge and all your hair will be caught in the net.

Second, if you must have a lace-front wig, buy one that does not need to be glued down. I know many will say you must do this, but you don't have to if you find the right one and adjust the inner bands enough so that it stays snug, but doesn't creep back on your head. I never wear glue with my Arda lace-front, just two hair pins on either side near the ears, and it stays put perfectly, looking very natural.

Third and most importantly, treat your hair well when you're off the job, especially you women with long hair! After a weekend of parties, I do a deep-conditioning treatment on my hair, which involves mixing up half a cup of olive oil, a few drops of tea tree oil (which is a great anti-fungal and anti-bacterial oil for treating your scalp and also balances the oil levels to make it less oily) and a little bit of honey. Whisk together and put it on your hair over the *sink* (not in the bathtub, or you'll create a slippery mess that will be dangerous to the next person who steps in for a shower).

I bundle up that treatment under a dollar-store shower cap, wrap it in a towel to prevent leaks and let it sit for about an hour. I rinse it all out afterward, give my hair a good shampooing or two to get it all out, then condition. It leaves my normally frizzy and unruly hair perfectly smooth and soft! You can substitute coconut oil if you want something a bit less heavy.

Another mistake is in rubbing or turbaning your hair with a bath towel. Much as I recommend satin pillowcases to reduce friction and grinding of your hair follicles, bath towels are too harsh for delicate or damaged hair, even just for patting dry! An often-repeated bit of advice is to get an old, soft t-shirt and use that for a towel. Just tip your head over, insert your head in the bottom of it, stand up and flip the collar end onto the top of your head.

It stays put while soaking up excess water slowly and gently. It will not get your head perfectly dry, so after about 20 minutes, take it out and detangle with a very wide comb, then let your hair air-dry.

And on that note ladies, *don't ever brush wet hair.* Your hair is most fragile and prone to snapping and breaking after it's just been washed. A brush will snap strands and cause lots of breakage. Only use a wide-tooth comb, and only after you've blotted out the excess water! Sleeping on wet hair, or sleeping with a ponytail, bun or braid in, will also do damage to the follicle and ends. A loose satin scarf is always best for sleeping.

Putting up wet hair inside a wig is also a terrible idea, not just for the aforementioned reasons, but because it can create a fungal infection in your scalp and make your wig smell bad. It may make your hair fit more easily under the wig, but it's just asking for trouble in the form of infection.

And as I always advise, sleeping with a satin pillowcase instead of a cotton one will help you out tremendously. They're not expensive and they smooth and protect your hair and skin at night!

These are just a few things you can do to prevent costume wear and tear on your body. Remember to take good care of yourself, so you can enjoy a long career as a character performer!

SECTION FOUR: EMERGENCY INDEX

From an emergency on-the-go kit to an alphabetical index of problems on the job, this section will get you through almost any professional emergency!

Your Emergency Kit

No matter what level you're at in this business, there's one thing you should never be without: your emergency car kit. Your kit is easy to put together and hard to work without. Putting one together and stashing it in your vehicle before your first gig should be a high priority, because there are constant last-minute fixes that you will deal with in this line of work.

A medium-sized zippered makeup bag or a pencil bag is ideal, but any small, waterproof bag with a zipper will work. Make sure it's small enough to be stashed in your glove compartment, under the passenger seat or other convenient place.

Inside your bag should be:

   15 hair pins, blond and brown
   A tube of latex-free eyelash glue
   20 safety pins and a tiny sewing kit with scissors
   3 thin rubber bands
   10 medium latex-free bandaids
   A small comb
   A brown-black eyeliner pencil
   A pencil sharpener
   A tube of red lip gloss
   A cheap compact of face powder
   Oil-absorbing sheets
   2 dollars in quarters

Hair pins, safety pins and rubber bands are all extremely useful fasteners to fix torn, loose or broken costume pieces. A comb is great for last-minute hair and wig touch ups.
Eyelash glue, lip gloss and eyeliner are not just for princess or female characters . . . a good eyeliner pencil can be used to touch up pirate makeup, facial stubble, eyebrows, or draw any lines you need in a hurry, like a last-minute mustache. Red gloss can be used on your lips (for all those times you smudge

your lipstick off right before a party), but also rubbed into cheeks if you forget your blush. A powder compact will cover up any shine, sweat and blemishes in a pinch. Oil-absorbing sheets can be found at any drugstore and will take a lot of shine and oil off your face instantly, which is especially useful on a hot summer day, when you're between gigs and don't want to look shiny for pictures.

Lip gloss is preferable to lipstick, as the lipstick is likely to melt in your car if it gets hot, but the lip gloss will stay contained. And while eyelash glue will deteriorate over time in a hot car, it's worth it to replace it when needed, because you can use it to touch up lashes, fake facial hair, etc. A latex-free blend will not go bad as fast as latex and you can lend it to some other performers who may have latex allergies, so look for latex-free if you can. The same goes for the band aids, as you'd be surprised how many people have a latex sensitivity and it pays to just have an all-purpose bandage for everyone.

The quarters are for parking meters, which you will most certainly encounter for city gigs and which no one ever remembers money for.

It's important to point out that your emergency kit is for just that, *emergencies*. It shouldn't be used until you actually need it. Check it once a month to make sure all the contents are still good and remember to immediately replenish any items you use. It's an indispensable part of your job and when an emergencies strikes, you'll be very glad to have it!

One non-essential thing you can nevertheless consider having in your car is an EZ-Pass, or other regional electronic toll item. Sometimes you end up going through unexpected tolls and forgetting to bring enough money for them and that's always the *worst* when you're in a big hurry to a gig. A toll electronic pass is a great item to have, since it's hooked up to your bank account and will automatically bill you for the amount, so you can cruise though the electronic pass lane and avoid lines in cash lanes.

I also like to have a wig cap, a pair of socks and a generic pair of white short gloves floating around my car somewhere. When you're a princess, you have a ton of accessories to keep track of for each costume, and a pair of gloves usually gets left behind. It's better to have a pair of generic white gloves ready, just in case. As for the socks: a lot of gigs take place at bounce house facilities and children's play places, where the house rule is "socks only" and no shoes are allowed in the play area. That rule almost always applies to the performer as well, so a clean pair of socks is nice to remember, in case your pirate, princess, fairy or other character has nylons on instead of regular socks. This rule doesn't apply to mascot characters.

If your particular character has a specific item that you know you will definitely not be able to do without, it's a good idea to put one or two spares in your trunk. Here are just a few suggestions for specific performers:

MASCOTS

A spare towel
Deodorant
Spare sneakers
A sweatband

PRINCESSES

Spare tiara or crown
Pair of long gloves
Pair of neutral-colored flat shoes

HEROES

Athletic cup
Spare mask (domino-style with elastic)

PIRATES

Bandana
Extra belt
Box of plastic gold coins (you lose a few of these at every
          party)

151

The Party Princess Handbook

Emergency Index

If you're on the job, just getting ready or just about to leave, random problems will undoubtedly come up. Bring this book with you to gigs and consult the following emergency index for solutions to common crises that performers may face.

Keep in mind that a great many of these emergencies can be easily avoided by adhering to the advice in the previous emergency car kit section, researching routes and weather beforehand and by having your vehicle regularly serviced. The best way to solve problems is by making sure they never happen in the first place!

The Party Princess Handbook

Section i. Before the party

Acne breakout

Do not pop pimples or try to lance with needles or foreign objects. Apply an ice cube to the inflammation and keep it there until it melts (about 5 minutes). It'll sting for about a minute, but will become numb shortly after, leaving a reddened area that will fade in about twenty minutes. If there is no visible redness from the blemish itself, apply foundation, then use a good skin-colored concealing product and set with powder. If reddened, apply some eye drops like Clear Eyes to reduce the redness, then apply makeup. Quite often, people will notice the acne far less than you do.

Allergies

If you have prescription medication for allergies, take it. If driving yourself to the party, do not take over-the-counter drugs which may make you drowsy. If allergies are going to interfere with your work, call boss and ask for a replacement.

Cold or flu

Call your boss and ask for a replacement. Do not work a party when you're sick, no matter how much of an emergency it is.

Costume doesn't fit

Weight gain/loss: Use safety pins to adjust, pinning from the inside along the natural side seams of the costume. If waist is loose, put on two tank tops underneath the costume to pad it out and tie a colorful sash or bit of fabric around your waist to cinch it. If weight gain prevents costume from zipping up in the back, zip it as far as it will go and add a decorative short cape to cover it, or have a friend pin a strip of matching colored fabric down your back, just covering the zipper and exposed middle. Use straight pins for this, not safety pins, as they will be less visible. Be careful not to poke yourself while performing. Call your boss if costume is still unusable.

Too short/tall for dress: Too short: roll up the costume at the waist and safety pin from the inside. Fold up sleeve cuffs from the inside. Add tall shoes for dresses so they clear the ground. Too tall: wear flat shoes. If in pants, wear boots to cover the ankles. If the sleeves are too short, add big bracelets for female characters or pirates, or wear a longer sleeved shirt underneath.

Wig too big/small: For loose wigs, make sure the elastic hooks in the back inside of the wig are hooked onto the little loops of the inner headband. If the wig is really loose, connect the hooks directly to each other and hair pin wig carefully. If a wig is too small, apply it as far as it will go onto your head in the front. Tie a sparkly or colorful headband or bit of fabric across the top of your head and knot it carefully in the back to cover where your natural hairline shows. Use LOTS of hair pins to keep wig in place, especially along the front hairline.

Eye irritation/infection

If eye is red with irritation, use anti-red eye drops like Clear Eyes and apply less eye makeup, staying away from pencil liners or mascara close to the lash root. If eye is infected, apply a warm compress to soothe swelling and redness. Wipe eye clear of debris and apply eye drops. Do not apply makeup to the eye. If eye's appearance is too obvious, call boss and ask for replacement. Do not work a party with pink eye, as it is easily passed to children.

Family emergency

If a family or personal crisis occurs, call boss for a replacement. If it happens within one hour of the event or a replacement can't be found, you may be required to work regardless. If it's truly dire, your boss may cancel on the client, but this is an absolute last-minute resort, only for very serious emergencies.

Missing costume pieces

If missing jewelry, substitute with anything similar you own, or leave off. If missing shoes, wear neutral-colored or black shoes. If missing gloves, props or other pieces, leave off. A missing costume piece does not always make or break the visual effect. Do not try to explain away the missing piece to children at parties. Gloss over it and it will likely not be noticed.

Skin Injury: visible cut, scrape, rash

If injury is superficial but will be visible to children, cover with long gloves, a sash, or wear a matching long-sleeved shirt under your costume. Do not apply a big visible bandaid. If necessary, get a large glitter sticker that matches your outfit and apply it over that spot. For pirates, apply a fake tattoo. If spotted and asked by children, explain that you got a bump when you fell off your horse while out on a ride.

Sore throat or voice gone

Do not take liquid cold medicine, but instead go for a bag of cough drops with honey in them. Remove singing from your repertoire and substitute activities that don't require a lot of talking, like crafts and freeze dancing. Encourage children to talk by asking them questions about themselves, sharing stories about their pets or their schools. Take along your boom box and CDs of music. If parents insist on singing, encourage a singalong with the CD track and let the recorded music cover up your own voice. Do not work with a serious sore throat as it may be contagious.

Sunburn

Apply aloe vera as early as possible. When getting ready, apply sunscreen and powder over with very light facial powder. Do not apply heavy concealer or foundation, as it will stain the costume and sweat off quickly.

Section ii. In the car

Broken zipper

Repair with safety pin or cover with cloak or sash. If you have a host present, they may be able to sew it closed for you temporarily.

Broken heel

Remove broken heel. If feet are obscured by a large dress, walk with one heel in the air. If not, use other shoes, even street shoes. If nothing else works, try to break the heel off the remaining shoe so they match.

Flat tire

Call parent immediately and let them know the situation, and that you will be a bit late. Call boss and repeat this info. To change a car tire, consult the manual in your car, usually in the glove compartment. All tools and a small jack should be in with the spare tire in the trunk. Determine if your car has a wheel lock first, before attempting to remove the wheel. For faster progress, call up "How to Change on Tire" on WikiHow on your smartphone and follow the 14 steps with pictures. It's not as hard as it seems.

Do not attempt to change a tire in a ballgown or other dress. Change into spare clothes or ask boss to come and meet you to help. If possible, have a membership in AAA or other road service.

Late to Hub

Call and let boss know you're en route.

Late to party/traffic/roadblock

Call client and let them know you have hit some unavoidable traffic, but are on your way. Offer to start a few minutes late and stay a few minutes late. Call boss and let them know as well. Don't speed to make the party, or you may be pulled over and delayed even further.

Lost

No one should get lost in this day of smartphones and GPS units, but in case you are, call your boss and ask for directions immediately. If that's not possible, pull over to the nearest gas station and ask for directions. Someone there should have a smartphone on them. When you recover your route, call the client and let them know if there will be a delay in your arrival.

Missing lipstick/blush/other makeup

Substitute lipstick for blush by dotting along cheeks and rubbing in. Rub blush or pink shadow into lip balm to make emergency lipstick. If no face powder, blot face on oil sheets or tissue to take shine off. For darkened eyebrows, strike a match and blow it out, then wait for it to cool. Use the burned edge to powder in new brows. If no mascara, use lip balm or lip gloss on eyelashes to make them look wetter and darker, doing both top and bottom lashes.

No place to change

If you can't change in your vehicle, find the nearest gas station, supermarket or fast food location. As a last resort, ask an office building to use their bathroom and tell them why. Emphasize child's birthday will be ruined if you don't change soon.

No parking

Call parent and let them know you're still looking for parking. They may know a good spot or have a place on their property where you can park. If nothing else presents itself, park at a gas station as far to the side and back as possible. Run into the station and ask them if you can leave your car there for a little bit. Don't tell them how long the party is, just say "a little bit." You'll be good to go as long as they say yes.

Parent doesn't answer phone

Leave a voicemail message and try an alternate number, then call boss to let them know. The parent may be trying to call the boss by mistake. If no answer when calling before entering the home, knock on the door at the appointed time regardless. Parent may have accidentally turned their phone off.

Pulled over (police)

If pulled over while speeding/making an illegal turn, apologize immediately and tell the officer it's your fault for not being more aware. Explain that you're on your way to a child's birthday party. Don't beg to be let off or let go on warning, just wait for their response. They may decide to let you off, or they may not. At any rate, call the parent as soon as you are let go and let them know you had traffic trouble and were held up, but are on your way ASAP.

Sweating, outside of party

Use oil sheets to blot moisture off face without taking off makeup. Crank the AC in your car and let it blow inside your costume to dry it out.

Torn or dirty costume

Call boss to see if you can return to Hub in time to change, or get another host or performer to drive a new costume to your location. If not, do the party as-is and try to keep that part of your costume obscured as much as possible. Do more seated activities like singing and storytelling, which don't show off your costume as much.

Weather conditions

If weather is inclement, allow extra time for driving and call client to alert them to the bad driving conditions. Do not speed to make the party. If tornado, hurricane or other dangerous conditions occur, call the boss and ask them to advise. You may have to turn back and the party will be rescheduled. If there's rain or snow and you have no umbrella, use a sheet of paper or whatever is handy and remember to cover your wig first before anything else, as it gets wrecked in water the fastest. If you're a princess, try flipping your large skirt inside-out over your head, to cover your wig and keep the outside of the dress a little more dry.

Section iii. At the party

Allergies

Keep a tissue handy up your sleeve, tucked into a glove or inside bodice of costume. Pretending to laugh into a handkerchief is also a good cover for wiping your nose or eyes. If children notice, explain it with an in-character reason (prince/princess/fairy: "I got sprinkled with fairy dust today and it makes me sneeze!" Pirate: "I'm allergic to all this land, I wish I was back at sea!" Superhero: "Someone here must have superpowers . . . I can always sense them when I sneeze!")

Additional company, booked

Report to your boss about any other character company present at the event. Cooperate with the other performers and ask your boss to advise you on whether to do group pictures or not. Otherwise, work with other performers as you would with your own company.

Additional company, talent not up to standards/behaving badly

Try to distance yourself from the other's company's performers without ruining the event for children. Stay on the opposite side of the event from the other performers to avoid being in pictures or groups with them. If necessary, pull them aside and quietly correct them on bad behavior. Report any bad behavior to your boss, just in case.

Adults, acting inappropriately

Adults at parties who are acting inappropriately towards the performer should be corrected in private by the host or hostess, never by the performer. If absolutely necessary, the performer can quietly inform the parent or client who booked them, and let them correct the other adult themselves. If a performer ever feels unsafe or threatened, they should have the right to leave the party, no questions asked. Discuss this with your boss before accepting your first assignment.

Adults, breaking illusion

Correct adults who call you out as an actor by saying, "Oh no, you must have me mistaken for one of my friends! I'm (character name)!" Be insistent no matter what, and do not break character. If the adult is belligerent or ruining things for the children, try to alert host or client to the situation to have that adult removed from earshot of children.

Adults, drunk and harassing performers

The host or hostess should immediately make their concerns about drunk adults clear to the parent or client. If there's no host, you have the right as a performer to quietly broach the topic with the client, out of earshot of children.

Adults, too loud

Adults interfering with the activities by making too much room noise should be shushed by the children in a game setting. Try the following dialogue to the children: "Oh, it's SO loud in here! Can we all play the shush game and get the room really quiet? On the count of three, everybody yell SHUSH as loud as you can!" Keep repeating this game until the adults get the message.

Birthday child, forgot name

If you forgot the birthday child's name upon entering the party, immediately greet the children and say, "Can we all wish a very happy birthday to our special birthday boy/girl on the count of three?" The children will fill in the name of the birthday child automatically.

Birthday child, shy/unhappy

If the birthday child is shy, do not single them out in front of other children. Ask them if they'd like to sit next to you during some quiet, sit-down games and activities and address them only occasionally. Shy children often just want to be next to you, not make conversation. If the child is unhappy, offer him or her the choice of next activities, giving a list of up to three things to do and letting the child choose. If they are clearly scared of the performer, ask if they'd like mom or dad to sit next to them during activities and call the parent over.

Birthday child, tantrum

If the birthday child has a tantrum, treat it like a guest tantrum. Alert the parent immediately by saying, "Oh my, do you miss your mommy/daddy? Don't worry, they're right here!" and go get the parent to deal with the situation.

Costume piece missing, obvious

If an important costume piece is missing, i.e., wings on a fairy, try to improv a good reason for it. "My wings are invisible when I'm on earth" or "I didn't wear my crown because (birthday child's name) is the *real* birthday princess today!" are good stock responses.

Dog or other pet at party

If a dog or other pet is causing a problem, exclaim in your nicest tone, "Looks like our little friend wants to go into the other room for a while! Can anyone help him get there?" Give a look to the parent to let them know to remove the pet and secure it somewhere out of the way.

163

Kids, tantrum

If a child guest is having a tantrum and parents are present, try to ignore it and address the rest of the children. The parents will usually take the initiative in removing/calming the child. If no parent is present and the tantrum is ruining the other children's enjoyment of the party, ask the child if they would like to go see mommy or daddy. Take them by the hand and gently lead them to the nearest adult. State in a kind but firm tone that the child really wants to see his/her mommy or daddy and hand the child off to the adult. Then return to entertaining.

Kids, too old

If children are too old for your planned entertainment, switch up activities and do more talking and story games. Try to engage them in talking about their own lives, school activities and favorite things, as older kids love to talk about their own spheres of interest.

Kids, too scared

If children are too afraid of the entertainer, get the host to run interference and talk them down. Stay low to the ground and do not make sudden moves or large gestures. Talk softly and encouragingly. Invite a parent over to "meet" you, so children can see that the adult is safe with you and you pose no threat. Do not attempt to make physical contact with the children. Turn on ambient music and encourage dancing, so children can keep their distance from you while still participating. Eventually, they should warm up to you.

Kids, too young

If children are too young for your activities or will not hold still for stories and singing, switch over to dancing, freeze dance, musical chairs, Simon Says and other active, but simple, games.

Kids, violent/roughhousing the performers

If children become too violent or rough with the performer, you have the right to protect yourself. Step away from entertaining and quietly inform the parent that it is their duty to intercept any badly-behaving children and take them aside for quiet time. If the children continue to rough the performer, give the parent a second private warning and inform them that you will leave if the bad behavior continues. If the client refuses to get involved, inform the children that you had a wonderful visit and hope to come back soon, then promptly leave and inform your boss by text or phone.

No answer at door

If no one answers the door when it's time to enter the house or event, double-check the address and then call the client on the phone. Leave a message if they don't answer, stating that you are now entering. Open the front door cautiously and try to subtly get the attention of the nearest adult. Tell them to find and inform the client of your arrival. Wait outside until the client meets you.

No music (CD broken, can't plug in)

Do not admit to children that the music player is broken or music is not available. Tell them that you just had a great idea and want them to "make music" by clapping along while freeze dance or musical chairs are played. Encourage clapping, jumping and dancing, and yell "FREEZE!" when you want them to stop. Cajole parents into helping you clap along. Switch any further dancing or music games to story time and singing.

No room to perform

If there is no room to perform active games in the house, switch over to seated activities like story time, guessing games, singalongs, and acting out stories with your hands. Tell a story and encourage the children to use hand movements to help make the story come alive (wiggly fingers for bugs, falling rain, flapping hands for birds, etc.).

Outdoor/non-air conditioned party without consent

Politely ask the parent if the party is being held indoors as agreed upon. If they disagree, perform the party and inform your boss immediately after. However, if your party includes a mascot character, politely insist that the entertainment MUST take place indoors or the performer may suffer heat stroke.

Supplies/crafts run out/too many guests

If there are far more guests than the client estimated, make sure you have extra supplies. If you don't have enough, do not do crafts, as it will lead to squabbling. Substitute a freeze dance or other group activity. If the parent complains later, politely inform them that you only brought enough crafts for the amount of children that they reported as being in attendance. Refer them to your boss if they're still unsatisfied.

Sweating, inside the party

If you begin to sweat through your costume, minimize your movements and switch to seated or stationary activities. If dancing, stand in one place and wave to children as they dance, shouting instructions or encouragements as needed. Switch to picture time as soon as you feel a bit cooled down, so as to get photos out of the way before you sweat any further.

Talkative child/children

If a child is monopolizing your attention or interrupting constantly, give them plenty of eye contact to let them know that you are paying attention to them. Always acknowledge their questions with a "Yes!", even if you don't fully answer them. Invite them to sit on your lap during stories or songs and gently hold their hands in yours, to keep them from being tempted to stand and interrupt again.

Wrong character showed

If the wrong character was dispatched to a party, apologize for the mix-up to the client or have the host apologize and call the boss, who may want to offer a discount or free party to make up for it. If the children were expecting another character, tell them that the expected character had an unexpectedly busy day doing _____ and sent you along to say hello and meet everyone. Continue with the party as planned. Apologize again at the end to the client and be sure the boss has made contact with them to make amends. If the boss can't be reached, tell the client that your company prides itself on customer satisfaction and will be very happy to make it up to them, and that your boss will be contacting them shortly.

Wig pulled off/fell off

There's very little you can do if your wig comes off. Hopefully, it was a mere sliding of the wig and can be quickly grabbed and readjusted with minimal notice. If it's a full-on wig loss in front of the children, laugh loudly and do a hammed-up "WHOOPS!" about it, replace the wig, then ask them if *their* hair ever wants to sneak away and dance at parties. Keep deflecting with other unrelated questions about them, until the incident is forgotten. Apologize to the client at the end of the party, just in case.

Section iv. After the party

Costume has been stained/ripped/ruined

Inform the boss immediately, especially if it must be used again that day by another performer. If it's needed that day and there's still time, find another employee who can sew and do what mending you can.

Dissatisfied parents

Do not attempt to argue with unhappy clients after a party,

but refer all concerns to your boss and hand them a business card. Be polite and accommodating at all costs, but leave the actual arguments and negotiations to your employer.

Follow-up complaint to boss/bad online review

Unfavorable reviews are inevitable, even for top-tier companies. If it's about you personally, discuss with your boss what went wrong at the event and what you can improve. Do not automatically blame the client for being unreasonable; however, if you feel their review was unfair, explain your side of it to your boss.

Forgot party supplies/equipment at client's house

Call the client and apologize, informing them that something was left at their residence. Inquire as to what would be a convenient time for you to return to pick it up. Inform your boss as well, as she may advise you to leave a coupon or other discount card with them when you retrieve the items.

No tip

Do not ever ask outright for a tip. If you aren't offered one, leave politely. Often a client will forget to tip, but may include one later in a check to your boss for the booking balance.

Parents won't pay balance

If a balance payment is expected at the end of the party and a parent refuses to pay, call your boss and ask how to proceed. Leave the house, but do not leave the area until you have spoken to your boss or a senior employee about what to do.

In Closing

I hope this handbook has really helped you in your journey towards joining the ranks of one of the silliest, weirdest, most demanding and most fun professions I've ever had the pleasure of putting on my business cards. After reading through this book, you may feel a bit overwhelmed by just how much work is involved in party performing. But hopefully you've also realized just how many possibilities are open to you now and how much potential you personally have to make a difference in a little friend's day.

If you still have questions or want more advice, feel free to message me on my blog at ThePrincessForHire.com. I'm always available to help out with any questions you might want answered.

And always remember that at the end of the day, it's not what you do for a living that matters, but whether or not you had fun doing it. Life's short, so make every day a special party!

ACKNOWLEDGEMENTS

Thanks to all of the generous backers who donated their money, time and efforts into funding this book through Kickstarter and spreading the word about this project. None of this would have been possible without your support and kindness. You're the *real* royalty!

A Walsh
Adam Shaughnessy
Adam Trahan
Alanna Sadgrove
Alex
Alexander Li
Alexandra Abene
Alice
Amanda Reeves
Amanda Seferian
Andi Scott
Andrea Ales
Anna Hagerty
Anonymous
Ardella
Ashley Galinato
Athena Michelle
Beth Cosby
Bonnie Ahrens
Brett Mount
Brian Eng
Bridget Wilde
Bridgette A.
Brittany
Brittany Bowman

Brooke Fencl
CC
Camille Trejo
Carl Patten
Carla
Caroline
Carrie Martin
Catherine Caine
Catherine Callaghan
Charlene Harrison
Cheshire
Christian Wilson
Christine Maurette
Christine McLeod
Chrystie Goody
Claire Rudolph
Dael Jackson
Daggerdragon
Dan Nagle
Dan Stryker
Daniel Forrest Ross
Daniel Lindquist
Dave Agnew
David E. Smith
David Patricola

Dawn
Denise Devlin
Diana
Dominique Brooks
Drucilla Shultz
Dustin Javier
EAK
Elii
Emily Barratt
Emily Baumann
Erik Hinrichsen
Erika
Evan Gautama
Frances Penington
Geoff Upton-Rowley
George F Comstock
Gene Gruenenfelder
Hannah Lorber
Hannah Thoo
Hapsetshut
Heather Lee Dixon
Dragulescu
Heather Stevenson
Hilary Jana
Holly Golightly
JBai
Janne Johnsen Blakstad
Jeddie
Jeff Kapustka
Jennifer Senate
Jenny Newman
Jeremiah Shilling
Jess Lethbridge
Joe Saturday
Johanna Pabst
John Schmidley
Jonathan Kerry
Jordana Robinson
Kailee Coll

Karen
Karlie Higgins
Karyn Moynihan
Kate
Katherine
Kathryn H. Awesome
Kathryn Johnson
Kathryn Kerr
Kathryn Tewson
Katie Laczko
Katrina MacNamara
Kaydee Stratis
Kayt O
Kim S
Kimberly Ehlers
Krys Lewis
LMEbert
Lada Bordewick
Lara P Arnold
Lara Sheridan
Laura
Laura Wallace
Lauren Mich
Lauren Pitz
Leonard Frankel
Leyna Hamasaka
Lia Perrone
Libby Wentz
Lionel Pryce
Lisa Dettmer Illenberg
Liza
Maggie
Mai
Mallorie Siano
Marc Gagnon
Marissa Volkening
Martin
Marvin V.
Mary McDowell

Mattea LeWitt
Megan H
Megan Poje
Meghann Barry
Melissa
Melissa Cheu
Melissa Chinnock
Melissa Negron
Melodie McCutcheon
Michael Fowler
Michael Wawrzyniak
Michelle
Michelle Stulberger
Mike Smith
Mike VanHelder
Molly Irma Sexton
Morgan
Mr. Bean
Nellie Kitchen
Neonchameleon
Nethead Jay
Nich DiCaprio
Nicole
Nicole Whitehead
Niels
Noelle Borman
Oliver Oberg
Olivia Diaz
Paul Munday
Paul hackett
Paula Colen
Pebbles McWhorter
Penny Hutchinson
Poppy Carpenter
Prettiest Princess Games
Rachael Lippmann
Rachel Chapman

Rachel Grinti
Rachel Hullett
Rachel Kozlowski
Reading Owl
Rebecca Hannah
Rebecca Huntley
Rebecca Nardi
Renate Elster
Renniamh
Rob Speed
Robin Ray
Robin Zalek
Robyn Hazekamp
Robyn Markle
Samalander
Samantha
Sara Dunn
Sara Siemers
Sarah Bennett
Sarah Haag
Sarah Standinger
Serephita
Shiyiya
Sophia Owens
Sorcyress
Steph
Stephani Brodjieski
Steven G Saunders
Susie Hastie
Teagan N
Thanee Rongratana
Tyne Bloomfield
Victoria Belmont
Victoria Sueno
Wendy Bristow
Will Hall

About The Author

M. Alice LeGrow is a princess-superhero-fairy-pirate-mascot by day and a comic book writer by night Her party work has been profiled on NPR's *All Things Considered*, The Huffington Post, The Washington Times and in various other media.

When she's not busy getting in and out of costume, she runs the illustrated party character industry blog *How Wonderful!* at www.ThePrincessForHire.com.   And when she's not doing *that*, she's busy arguing with her cats.